TRADITIONAL JUDO

E G BARTLETT

SUMMERSDALE

Summersdale Publishers
46 West Street
Chichester
West Sussex
PO19 1RP
United Kingdom

A CIP catalogue record for this book is available from the British Library.

Printed and bound in Great Britain by Selwood Printing Ltd.

ISBN 1 873475 79 9

Other books by E G Bartlett

JUDO AND SELF DEFENCE (Thorsons 1962)
SELF DEFENCE IN THE HOME (Thorsons 1967)
BASIC JUDO (David & Charles 1974)
BASIC KARATE (Faber & Faber 1980)
WORLD OF SPORT - JUDO (Wayland 1988)

ACKNOWLEDGEMENTS

The demonstrations in this book are being given by Clifford Johnson, Clive Gardiner, Marc Thomas, Wendy Ivins, Kevin Morris, Ronald Morris and the author.

Photography is by Ronald Morris, Kevin Morris and Wendy Ivins.

Line Drawings are by Paul Jordan.

The author's thanks are due to all the above, and to the Teachers and the many practice-partners who have helped him on "the way" over the past 46 years.

CONTENTS

INTRODUCTION

Judo originated from the martial art of ju-jitsu. This art was taught in secret and practised non-competitively, as it relied on the element of surprise when used against those who did not know the movements. In the latter part of the nineteenth century, Dr Jigoro Kano, a Japanese educationalist, studied at a number of ju-jitsu schools, and selecting the best movements from each, he formulated a system that could be practised safely as a means of physical training and as a sport. He founded his first club The Kodokan, in 1882, and called his system "Judo." This is the name by which the art is known throughout the world today.

He enunciated two basic principles: "Maximum efficiency - Minimum effort" and "Mutual Aid." His method thus retained the original ju-jitsu ideas that strength was not the deciding factor, but skill, and the whole purpose of practice was to help each other to become better physically and mentally, and hence better able to play a useful role in the community.

The tendency in the West has been to concentrate on the competitive aspect of judo, and with its inclusion in the Olympic Games, this tendency has been even more marked. Many masters feel that this has led to neglect of the more fundamental aspects of the study.

Some of the judo throws are depicted on a frieze on the walls of the Shaolin Monastery in China. This was founded in the sixth century AD, and the movements are taken from a series of exercises designed by the Abbot, Tamo, in order to fit the monks for their religious exercises. The fact that they formed an excellent self-defence system was secondary to that of promoting bodily fitness. Judo has this same basic aim.

Tze Han, an early Chinese martial arts master said:
"If you only practise fighting and not the skills, you will become decrepit in old age." In her introduction to her book "Judo - A Pictorial Manual" Pat Harrington 5th Dan writes: "I have felt for a long time that there is too much emphasis placed upon the Shiai or contest aspect of judo today, and not enough attention is given to the technical, kata, mental and spiritual aspects of judo." In a circular to members of his organisation, Kenshiro Abbe 8th Dan, founder of the Kyu Shin Do school of judo, wrote: "The meaning of Kyu Shin Do is not a specific series of mere techniques, but a method of applying such techniques to achieve a deeper understanding of this universe of ours. In this way we can attain harmony with our fellow men, and take a step to universal understanding."

Traditionally, judo is a method of self-defence, not involving great strength but depending on skill and on yielding to an opponent's attack in order to overcome him. At a deeper level it becomes a way of life, as the disciplines of practice and the spirit in which it is undertaken are extended into daily living. Knowledge of these traditional methods is preserved in the purest form in the katas, which are ritual demonstrations of sequences of movements.

Today, there seem to be two forms of judo: traditional judo and sport judo. In the latter weight training often forms part of the preparation. This was unknown in traditional judo, which did not have weight categories in competition, since the proper application of a technique should enable even a weaker man to overcome a stronger.

In this book we shall study traditional methods. We shall first look at the basic principles and the methods of falling, and then come to the katas. The first two are usually required in examinations for First Dan, and all of them will repay study, even by those whose main interest is contest, because frequent practice of the katas will make the reaction to danger automatic, and will give a deeper understanding of how judo works.

Moreover the benefit of studying these traditional methods will last for ever. Physically, health, fitness and co-ordination will be improved. Mentally, students will become more alert, and gain a deeper insight into the basic principles and into themselves and their fellow men. Spiritually, they will come to terms with their own aggression and see it replaced with concern for others.

Chapter 1

BASIC PRINCIPLES

There are a number of basic ideas you must absorb before you can practise traditional judo effectively. We shall look at each in turn.

POSTURE

The basic stance is upright, with the feet normal distance apart, looking at a point level with the eyes. The knees are slightly bent and you are relaxed.

Figure 1

From this, you can move into the defensive posture by simply bending the knees slightly and lowering the stomach forward. Do not lean forwards but remain upright. This lowers your centre of gravity and is often effective in preventing a throw being done on you. The defensive posture is also sometimes taken by spreading the feet slightly wider apart, so lowering the body, but never lean forwards or hold the opponent off with stiff arms, as this lays you open to attack.

Figure 2

BALANCE

In order that the weak may overcome the strong, balance and leverage are the fundamental principles that must be understood. Consider a person standing upright in the basic posture with his toes on a line. He can be compared to a ladder standing upright. If such a ladder is unsupported, it will fall either directly forwards or directly backwards; it will not fall diagonally in either direction. In the same way, the man's balance can be broken either directly forwards or directly backwards. If he advances one foot, however, his balance can no longer be broken directly forwards or directly backwards, because he can brace the front or rear leg to save himself. His balance must now be broken diagonally, by a pull or a push.

The principle is that balance can be broken either to the front or to the rear along a line at right angles to an imaginary line drawn through his feet. It follows that when a man is advancing, his moment of greatest weakness is when his feet come into line; that is, when the rear foot is brought level with the front foot. This will be seen in Nage No Kata.

Breaking the opponent's balance is one of the first moves in judo. It can arise through his own movements. For example, by yielding slightly to his push, you can bring him onto his toes, and just before he steps forward to save himself, he is off-balance, and the opportunity to throw him is there. It can also arise by your moving away from him and pulling gently. To unbalance the opponent in this way, your pull must be slight. If you pull too hard, he will simply step forward and regain his balance, before you can act to throw him.

NON RESISTANCE

Balance is bound up with non-resistance. If your opponent pushes you with both hands, and you remain where you are you are holding him up. But if you retreat, yielding to his push, you will bring him off balance and facilitate a throw.

Think of a lamp-post. If, when you leant against it, it was suddenly taken away, you would fall down. Again, if the opponent pulls you, and you stay where you are, or pull back, you are holding him up, but if you yield suddenly to his pull, you are putting him off balance to his rear.

LEVERAGE

Consider the principle of a lever. See Diagram A.
The effort is applied at E. The fulcrum (i.e. the point at which the lever turns) is F. The resistance is at R. Now the greater the distance from E to F, in relation to R to F, the more mechanical advantage you get, and the more effective the lever.

Diagram A

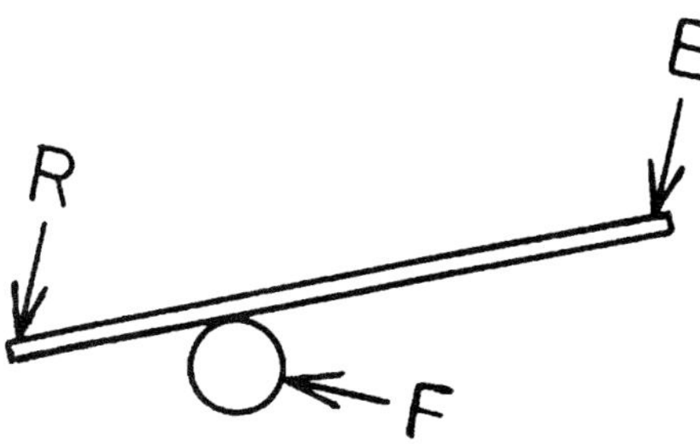

Applying this to the stomach armlock. Figure 134. The stomach is the fulcrum, F. The nearer the end of his arm that you apply pressure, pulling the elbow back against your stomach, the greater the effectiveness, and the less pressure you need to exert. Thus, a weaker person may be able to apply sufficient pressure to overcome a stronger one. The same principle applies in the Resisting Hip Throw, Tsurikomi Goshi, number 3 of the Hip Throws in Nage No Kata, Figure 20. The higher the pull with the thrower's right hand from his hip, the greater the leverage, and hence the greater the mechanical advantage.

MOVEMENT AROUND THE MAT

When moving forwards or backwards, do not cross your legs in the left-right action of ordinary walking. Slide one foot a pace forwards, bring the other up to half a pace behind, then slide the front foot forward again, and bring the other up to half a pace behind, thus progressing. To go backwards, slide the rear leg back a pace, and bring the front one back to half a pace behind. This movement is known as Tsugi-ashi.

Diagram B

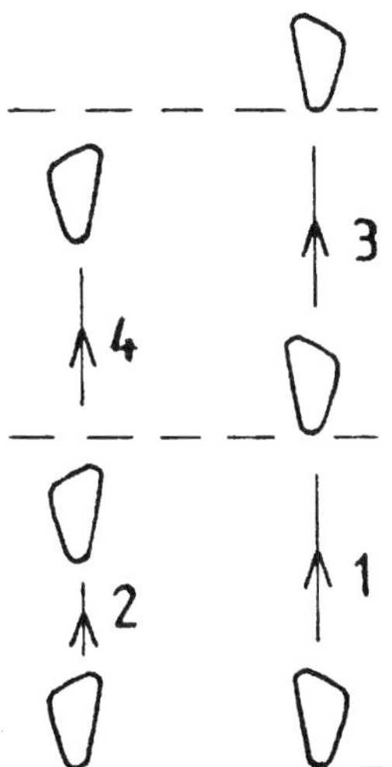

Keep the soles of the feet in close contact with the mat in all movements, sliding the feet, not picking them up as in ordinary walking. Keep the knees slightly bent. By moving in this way your centre of gravity will be kept low and you will be on balance and less open to a throw. Avoid crossing the legs, or bringing the feet too close together, as either facilitates a throw being done on you.

TURNING

When turning the body, as is needed for some movements and counters, think of your body as a door, hinged at one side, and turn as a door on this axis, either forwards or backwards. If, for example, you are turning on your right foot by taking your left back a quarter turn, and at the same time you are pulling your opponent forward with your left hand, then the force of your pull will be double what it would be if you turned about an axis through the centre of your body. In terms of the principle of levers, your effort arm will be the distance between your two sides, whereas if you turned about your centre, it would be half that.

When you turn, try to remain absolutely upright over the point on which you are turning. This movement is useful in many situations and as a counter move and is worth practising in itself. It is known as Tai Sabaki. See Diagram C.

It can be a quarter turn or a half turn as needed.

Diagram C

(i) **(ii)**

HOLDS ON JACKET

Judo is practised in a canvas jacket and trousers strong enough to stand up to wear. There are no buttons to injure either partner. The jacket is secured round the waist by a belt, wound round three times and tied in a reef knot in front. The reason these garments are worn is because if you were attacked in the street, it is likely your assailant would be clothed.

At the start of a practice or contest, opponents take the following holds on each other's jacket. With your left hand catch his right sleeve just under the elbow, and with your right hand catch his left lapel just under the collar bone. He will take the same holds on you. These holds are a starting point. They can be varied as necessary, for left-hand throws, for example, but to refuse to take hold can be a cause for disqualification. See Figure 3.

Figure 3

COURTESIES

Great store is set by courtesy in Judo. The hall where you practise is called the Dojo, and Dr Kano's first dojo was originally a Buddhist temple. The Dojo has always been treated as a near sacred place, a room dedicated to the study of the way. When you enter, you lay aside all thoughts of pride or anger. It is an oasis of peace, and you go there to help yourself and others to progress in the art. So you bow as soon as you enter, with the standing bow. See Figure 4.

Figure 4

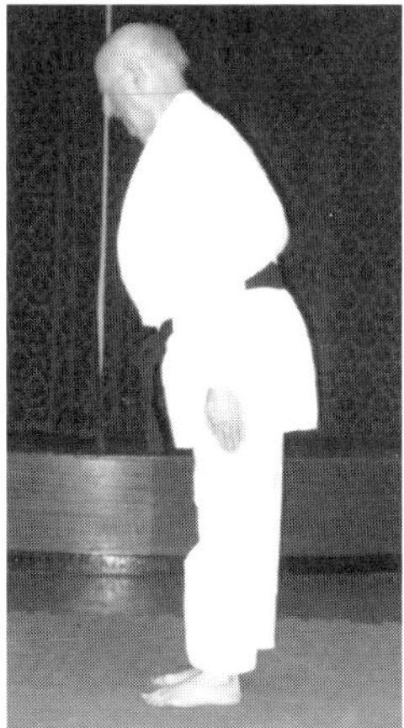

This bow is made with the heels together. Men allow their palms to slide down the sides of their trousers. Ladies can allow their palms to slide down the front of their thighs. The bow must be made gravely and sincerely, with due thought as to its meaning, and is slight (15deg from the vertical). This bow is also made to a partner before and after practice, when you step onto or off the mat, when the master speaks to you, or calls you forward for a demonstration, or if you ask him a question. It expresses deep respect. Remember that even if the person with whom you are practising is not as good as you are, he is giving up his time and doing his best to help you, simply by practising with you, and hence he is worthy of your respect.

At the beginning of a lesson, it is usual for the class to line up in order of grade facing the instructor and to make the kneeling bow (Rei) to him. In some clubs the senior student will give the command "Sensei Rei" (Bow to the Master); in others, both master and pupils simply kneel at the same time and bow. The kneeling bow is made in this way. Drop onto your left knee; then onto your right. Sit back on your heels, upright with your hands on your thighs. The tops of your feet should face the mat, the toes extended, and the big toes are crossed behind you. From this position, bend forward, and place both forearms on the ground, hands pointing inwards and about six inches apart, and lower your head so that the crown is towards whoever you are bowing to. See Figure 5.

Figure 5

These courtesies sometimes seem artificial to Western eyes, but judo is a way of life, and the etiquette of judo is all important. When you bow, you express your inner attitude of respect and friendship.

Chapter 2

BREAKFALLS

Breakfalls are the methods of falling without hurting yourself. Strangely enough they are no longer taught in some clubs, but they are an essential part of traditional judo and are needed in the demonstration of the katas, to which we shall come later in this book. Apart from their use in judo, they are an invaluable asset to anyone, even ordinary citizens.

The danger when we fall is that we will either put out a hand to save ourselves, or we will let our head flop back. The former can lead to a broken wrist, the latter to a fractured skull, particularly on hard ground. Breakfalls avoid both these dangers.

Apart from their value in enabling us to be thrown safely, breakfalls have a special use for those whose main interest is contest. If you are afraid of falling, you will fight very defensively, and defensive fighting rarely wins. If you know you can be thrown without harm, you can take risks and attack whole-heartedly.

The principle of break-falling is that we curl up in a ball as we land, and never put out a hand to save ourselves. There are four falls to be learnt, though as some are done to left and to right, this makes six in all.

1. The Side Breakfall

From a standing position, feet normal distance apart, raise your right leg parallel to the ground and cross your right hand over your chest.

Figure 6

Now lower yourself by bending your left knee, and sit as close to your heel as possible, immediately rolling back onto your shoulders and letting your feet come up. Look at your belt as you are doing this, as this will keep the back of your head from hitting the ground. Just as your shoulders are landing, strike the mat on your right side with the whole of your right arm, palm down, at an angle of 45^{0} to the body. The arm should be swung like a whip, not held stiffly like a stick.

Figure 7

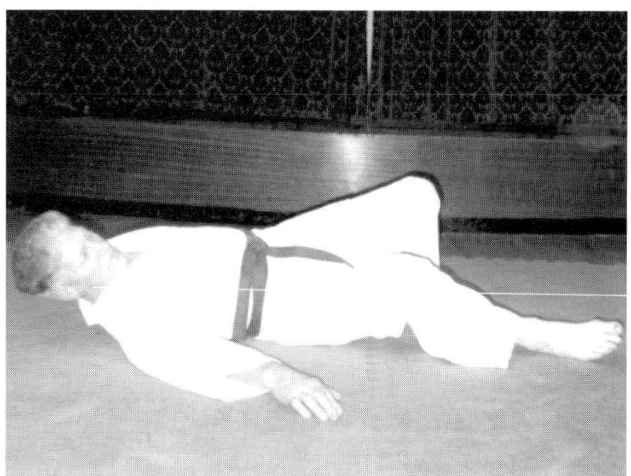

It is important to get the correct angle. Too near the body will result in your falling on the arm; too far away will cause shoulder injury.

This breakfall can also be done on the other side, by raising the left leg, and striking with the left hand.

2. The Backwards Breakfall

Start from the standing position with feet normal distance apart, as before, but this time cross both your arms over your chest. Sit close to your heels, and roll back, swinging both arms down to strike the mat on either side of the body at an angle of 45^{0}. The arms, if swung in the correct manner will bounce off the mat. Keep your knees apart, and remember to look at your belt throughout, to keep your head from flopping back.

Figure 8

3. The Shoulder Rolling Breakfall

Stand with the right foot forward. Bend down and place both hands on the mat, your right hand just in front of your right foot, fingers turned in, your left hand under your left shoulder, fingers turned in.

Figure 9

From here, push off with your left foot, tuck your head in, and roll directly forwards, head over heels. As you come over onto your back, strike the mat with your left hand in the side breakfall.

Again, you can do the breakfall on the other side, by starting with the left foot forward, and striking with the right hand.

4. The Forwards Breakfall

This is rarely used in judo, as the aim is to throw the opponent onto his back, not his face. It is learnt in case you are falling forward, but are too close to the ground to do one of the rolling breakfalls described above.

To practice, kneel down, upright, with your toes dug into the mat. Now, throw yourself forward onto your forearms and palms, with the fingers turned inwards, and raise your knees off the mat.

When you can do this, simply take a small jump from a standing position, landing on your forearms, palms, and toes, body stiff and straight. The object is to keep knees and nose off the mat, so that neither are injured. The position of landing is shown in the Figure.

Figure 10

Chapter 3

INTRODUCTION TO THE KATAS

Kata is probably one of the most neglected parts of judo training, particularly by those who see judo purely as a sport, but even for these, the study of Nage No Kata, Katame No Kata and Kaeshi Kata would have value. Dr Kano said that "In kata is to be found the spirit of judo, without which it is impossible to see the goal.."

Katas are a ritual sequence of exercises, in which one partner (Uke) gives the other (Tori) the perfect opportunity to perform a movement, be it throw, or hold, armlock, or defence. Sometimes the throw or lock will be in response to an attack by Uke. If this is so, then it must be a real attack. The kata must never be faked. Tori's application of the technique must be absolutely correct as regards timing, form and complete control of his partner. They thus work together to demonstrate the movements done under the most favourable conditions. The sequence of movements in any kata is unchangeable, and comprise a complete entity. Everything must be correct from first bow to last. Every movement and gesture must have its meaning, and there must be no unnecessary movement. Between each demonstration the performers must remain absolutely still.

When performed by skilled judoka, the katas have a beauty and a dignity that is impressive and akin to poetry of motion, but we may ask, "What is the practical value?" There are three main benefits to be derived from the practice of the katas:

1. In judo, you are trying to develop instinctive responses to situations of attack. If someone attacks you, you do not have time to think. You have to defend yourself automatically. How often have we done some simple act, on the spur of the moment, and then said "I couldn't do that again if I tried", and we couldn't. Our body has reacted without conscious thought. We aim to make our judo like that, and the only way to do so, is by repetition of the various movements. Kata gives this repetition under the best conditions. Hence in judo contest, if the opponent tries a throw, the counter move is already being done by us. And in real life, if we are attacked, constant repetition has made us move out of the way, or counter attack.

2. On the lowest level, knowledge of kata is required for grading examinations, in most organisations. Nage No Kata and Katame No Kata are required for Black Belt First Dan, and the others at higher level. Some organisations allow women to offer Ju No Kata as an alternative to contest.

3. But the most valuable benefit from kata training is the effect it has on the character of the performers. Kata requires concentration to make each movement accurate, co-operation to work in absolute harmony with your partner, courtesy and care for your partner so that you do not take advantage of the opportunity he is presenting to do him injury, even accidentally. The movements are made with dignity and require a discipline only developed by years of training. You are seeking gracefulness of movement. All these qualities, if assiduously sought after, will be eventually carried over into your daily living, and will make you more co-operative, thoughtful, helpful, courteous people.

In addition to these general benefits of kata practice, each has its own specific use. In Nage No Kata, most of the throws are done in response to an attack. Think of how valuable these techniques would be in the event of a real attack. In Katame No Kata, we are learning ways to immobilise an opponent or to make him submit to an armlock or stranglehold. This knowledge could be useful in case of real attack. In Kaeshi Kata, we are learning counter-throws. This would be useful to a contest-orientated student. In Ju No Kata, we are learning the basic ideas of balance and displacement, practising the simple quarter-turns (tai sabaki) that take us out of danger, when attacked, practising counter-moves, which, although not taken to their conclusion in the kata, none-the-less give us practice in making them, and develop grace and dignity of movement. In Kime No Kata, we are looking at self-defence, pure and simple.

One or more katas is often performed on ceremonial occasions, such as the opening of the dojo after a holiday, or in honour of a special guest. In such cases the guest and the masters would be seated at one side of the mat, often on a raised platform, and the place where they are sitting is known as the 'joseki'. Since the demonstration is in their honour, the performers bow to the joseki, before and after the kata, and try where possible not to turn their backs on it, in their demonstration. To begin with they are always twelve feet apart.

Tori always stands to the right of the joseki, and Uke to the left, as seen from the joseki, and the kata is performed along a straight line drawn between them.

IMPORTANT NOTE

In order that detail of each movement can be more clearly seen, the photographs in this book have been taken from different angles, sometimes from the other side of the kata line, which of course shows Tori on the left and Uke on the right, but it is important to remember that they do not change their position in this way.

Chapter 4

NAGE NO KATA

The first kata to be learnt is Nage No Kata. It was created by Professor Jigoro Kano himself, and consists of three hand throws, three hip throws, three foot throws, three sacrifice throws in which the thrower falls on his back, and three sacrifice throws in which he falls on his side. Each throw is demonstrated to left and to right, making thirty throws in all.

To begin Tori will stand to the right of the joseki, Uke to the left, as seen from the joseki. For a few seconds, they stand absolutely still and upright, facing each other, then they turn simultaneously towards the joseki, 45°, and make the standing bow, as described in Chapter 1. They then turn to face each other, and make the standing bow to each other. Each then steps forward left-right to bring their feet normal distance apart, ready for the first throw.

Visualise a straight line between them. This is the axis of the kata, and all throws are done down this axis. Most throws involve three steps being taken, each unbalancing Uke a little more until he is thrown on the third.

SET ONE (Hand Throws)

1. Uki Otoshi

Tori advances towards Uke with normal steps until he is near enough to take the normal holds. He must be upright, looking Uke straight in the face, and make no unnecessary movement such as swinging his hands. At the correct distance, he pauses a moment, before they simultaneously take the normal holds on each other's jackets. (See Chapter 1).

As they catch, Tori retreats with his left foot, and brings his right to within half a pace behind it, in the Tsugi-ashi movement described earlier. Uke is slightly unbalanced in a forward direction by this, and to regain his balance has to step forward with his right, and to follow it with his left, also in the tsugi-ashi movement. Their movements must be in perfect harmony.

Figure 11

Tori now repeats this movement, but this time taking a slightly longer step, so that he unbalances Uke a little more. Uke responds as before, thus regaining his balance.

When Tori retreats for the third time, he steps back a pace and a half with his left, turns his body to face directly across the line of the kata, and drops on his left knee. Note in so doing, his toes must be dug into the mat.

This is always so when executing a movement, unlike the kneeling bow, when the insteps are to the mat. Tori's body must be upright, and with his hands he makes a circular movement as though turning the wheel of a car, left hand pulling down and around, right lifting up, around and down. Uke, who was about to step forward as before, somersaults forward, down the line of the kata.

Figure 12

Uke lands with the side breakfall, already described. He gets up and walks to Tori's end of the kata line, and Tori arises and follows him. They now take the opposite hold, the left hand catching the lapel of the other, the right the sleeve. This time, Tori retreats with his right, and Uke follows with his left leading, until on the third step, Tori drops on his right knee, and performs the throw on the opposite side.

They arise and go to their own ends of the kata line. It is important that when arising and turning round, they try not to turn their backs on the joseki, but turn the other way, so that they are facing the joseki as far as possible. This is not always possible, however.

2. Seoi Nage

This is the second hand throw, and is in response to an attack by Uke. Tori advances with normal steps until he is about six feet away from Uke. Uke steps forward with his left foot, and takes his right arm behind him, ready to swing it up and over and to strike Tori on the top of his skull with the base of his clenched fist. This blow is one of the atemi or blows at vital spots that was practised in ju jitsu clubs. As he strikes the blow, he will bring his right foot forwards past his left, but Tori must bear in mind that his moment of greatest weakness is when his feet are in line, that is when the right is actually passing the left. Tori therefore synchronises his movements with those of Uke, and as Uke takes his arm back to strike, Tori turns and places his right foot just inside the point where Uke's right foot will be passing his left. Tori raises both his arms, and completely turns his back to Uke, by bringing his left foot back and inside Uke's left. He must not block Uke's blow with his hands, but allow it to pass between his arms.

Figure 13

He now catches Uke's sleeve with his left hand and throwing his right shoulder under Uke's right armpit, he catches his upper outer sleeve with his right hand. As he moves in to this position, Tori slightly bends his knees, and if he now straightens them, he will lift Uke onto his back and throw him over his right shoulder.

Figure 14

Uke's own impetus makes the throw very simple. He lands with a side breakfall along the axis of the kata, arises and goes to Tori's end where he turns round, ready to repeat the movement from that end. Tori follows him to a distance of six feet, and this time Uke advances his right foot and attacks with his left hand, to do the throw in reverse.

It is important that Tori supports Uke as he falls with his hold on the sleeve. Care of one's partner is part of the courtesy demanded of judo students, and it would be a disgrace if he were injured by your neglect.

3. Kata Guruma

This is the third of the hand throws. Tori approaches to a position where he can take the normal holds on Uke. They catch simultaneously, as Tori steps back with his left and Uke follows with his right, as in the first throw.
On their second steps, Tori changes his left hand hold on the sleeve, for a grip on the underside, palm upwards.

Figure 15

On his third step back with his left, Tori leaves his right where it is, and bending his knees, he places his right shoulder at Uke's right hip. At the same time, he thrusts his right arm between Uke's legs and grasps the back of his trousers, low down. Uke coming forward meanwhile has been drawn onto Tori's shoulders at the back of his neck in the "fireman's lift" position, and if Tori now brings his left foot back towards his right, straightening his legs, he will be able to lift Uke clear of the ground.

Figure 16

Once Uke is up, Tori takes him straight over, to fall at his left side along the line of the kata. This is a heavy fall, so practise with care to support Uke. When Uke arises, they go to Tori's end, and by reversing the holds and directions, perform the throw on the other side.

This marks the end of the first set, so there is a slight pause, as each goes to his own end of the kata line, and turning their back to the other, quietly adjust their jackets. They then turn to face each other ready for the second set.

SET TWO (Hip Throws)

1. Uki Goshi

Tori advances to within six feet of Uke. As with Seoi Nage in the last set, Uke advances his left foot and as he brings his right forward, he attempts to strike Tori on the top of his head with his right bottom fist. As he does so, he will advance his right foot. Again, Tori must remember that his moment of greatest weakness is when his feet are in line, that is when the right is passing the left. Tori turns in by taking his left foot forward and placing it just inside Uke's left, then bringing his right back to place just inside the spot where Uke's right foot will come. The blow goes over Tori's shoulder. He passes his left arm round Uke's waist at belt level, and with his right hand catches Uke's left sleeve at just below the elbow. Uke will hold his left hand slightly in advance to facilitate this. Tori bends his knees slightly as he moves in, and he will find that by straightening them, he is able to bring Uke onto his left hip.

Figure 17

From here a turn to the right by Tori will bring Uke over his hip to land in front of him, across the line of the kata.

Figure 18

Uke arises and goes to Tori's end. Tori follows. Uke now advances his right foot, and attempts to strike Tori with his left hand, and by reversing the directions above, Tori will throw him with the same throw on the opposite side.

2. Harai Goshi

This throw is performed from the three step movement as in Uki Otoshi. Tori advances close enough to take the normal holds. As they catch hold, he retreats with his left, Uke following with his right.

On the second step, Tori changes his right hand hold on Uke's left lapel, passing his hand under Uke's armpit to rest on the back of his right shoulder blade. At the same time he turns his back on Uke for a hip throw, by taking his left foot back and around.

On Uke's third step forwards, Tori is in position to raise his right foot from the ground, and with the whole of his right leg, to sweep against the outside of Uke's right, thus throwing him with the sweeping hip throw.

Figure 19

For the sweep, the contact is made between the upper part of Tori's leg and the thigh of Uke.

Uke arises, goes to Tori's end of the kata, and by reversing all directions, the throw is performed on the other side, bringing Uke back to his own end.

3. Tsurikomi Goshi

This is another three-step movement. Tori advances as before, and they take hold as he withdraws his left foot, closely followed by Uke advancing his right. On the second step, Tori takes his left foot back and around, so as to completely turn his back to Uke, and to be in a position for a hip throw. At the same time, he lets go Uke's lapel with his right hand, and takes a hold high on his left collar.

Figure 20

Uke now stiffens up, to resist being thrown, and this must be clearly demonstrated in the kata. To overcome this stiffening, Tori bends his knees much more, and pulls forward with his right hand, so as to bring Uke over his hip.

Figure 21

If Tori now continues to turn to his left, he will throw Uke across the line of the kata, in front of him.

Uke arises, goes to Tori's end, and they take the opposite holds, preparatory to performing the same throw in reverse.

This being the end of a set, they turn their backs on each other, pause, adjust their jackets, then turn to face each other for the third set.

SET THREE (Foot Throws)

1. Okuri Ashi Barai

Tori advances until close enough to take the normal holds. As they catch each other's jackets, he advances his left foot and turns to face across the line of the kata, and Uke takes his right foot back and does the quarter turn that brings him face to face with Tori. They are now facing each other at right angles to the axis of the kata.

Together they move to Uke's left, with swift movements. Uke moves his left foot first, and this time brings his right close up to it, a dangerous position which gives the opening for the throw. Tori keeps time with him, moving first his right foot, and then his left, but not bringing it quite up to his left. At the same time he lifts Uke onto his toes by turning both his wrists upwards, and thrusting his stomach forwards. On the second step he makes this lift more pronounced, so that Uke is tottering on his toes.

On the third step, he sweeps Uke's right foot into his left, with the sole of his own left foot, and Uke is thus swept clean off the ground, and falls in front of Tori.

Figure 22

It must be noted that the sweep is made with a straight leg, and the point of contact is very low down. Tori turns his left foot so that the sweep is made with the sole, and the right side of his foot is below the ankle bone of Uke's right leg.

They arise, and repeat the throw, moving towards Uke's right.

2. Sasae Tsurikomi Ashi

For this throw, Tori approaches as before, and as they take the normal holds, he retreats with his left, Uke following with his right, as in Uki Otoshi. Tori increases his step on the second, thus disturbing Uke's balance. As he brings his right foot back for the second time, he takes it a pace and a half and places it to the right of the kata line and facing inwards at an angle of 45°.

He is now in a position to block Uke's third right step, by stretching out his left leg and placing the sole against the front of Uke's shin-bone, low down.

Figure 23

Now, by turning his body to his left, he can bring Uke over his outstretched leg to fall in front of him.

Figure 24

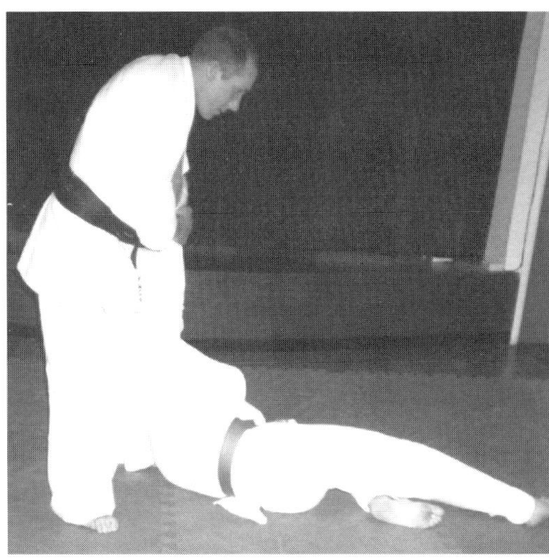

Uke arises, goes to Tori's end of the kata line, and they repeat the throw on the other side.

3. Uchi Mata

Both advance until they meet in the centre. They take the normal holds, but with their right hands a little higher up on the lapel. As the steps are apt to sound complicated, it is simpler if we think of the effect we are aiming at. Tori is going to take six small steps forwards, beginning with his left, and turning slightly each time to his right, so that by the time he has completed the sixth, he has made an about turn. Uke is going to take six large steps around the outside of Tori, beginning with his left, so that by the sixth step he would have gone right around Tori, and be back where he started.

To make him take these steps, Tori pulls with his right hand on Uke's left lapel, with a lifting pulling movement that compels him to move his left foot and then to bring his right around in order to keep his balance. Tori repeats this on the third and fourth steps.

When Uke makes his sixth large step, Tori does not take a step, but raising his right leg, sweeps the inner side of Uke's left thigh.

Figure 25

Uke is thrown in front of Tori. They arise, take the opposite holds, and repeat the throw on Uke's right leg by reversing the instructions.

As this is the end of a set, they return to their ends of the kata, for the usual pause and adjustment of jackets.

SET FOUR (Sacrifice Throws, falling on back)

1. Tomoe Nage

Tori and Uke approach until they meet in the centre of the mat, and take the normal holds on each other's jacket. Tori pushes Uke backwards, stepping forward with his right foot, then left. Uke retreats left-right. They retreat another step like this. On Tori's third advance, Uke resists, pushing back against him. Tori changes his left hand hold on Uke's sleeve to a hold on Uke's right lapel. Tori slides his left foot between Uke's legs, falls on his back, and brings his right foot up to place it against Uke's left hip bone. Now, by pulling down with his hands and straightening his right leg, Tori can lift Uke onto his foot, and by continuing the movement, can throw him over onto his back.

Figure 26

Uke has retreated left, right, left, right, left, right, but as Tori brings his right leg up for the throw, Uke advances his right foot, so as to do the right shoulder roll breakfall. When he has been thrown, he uses the impetus of his roll to come up on his feet, with his back to Tori. Tori arises; they turn round to face each other, meet in the centre of the mat, and repeat the movements from the other side. That is, Tori now advances his left foot, and Uke retreats with his right. Tori will thus throw with his left this time, and Uke will do the left shoulder roll.

2. Ura Nage

Tori advances until he is six feet from Uke. Uke raises his right arm to strike Tori on top of the head as in Seoi Nage. At the same time he steps forward with his left foot. Tori steps in with his left, and places his right hand, palm flat, in Uke's stomach, and catches his belt at the back with his left hand. Tori's right elbow rests on his right hip. As Uke delivers the blow, he brings his right foot forward. Tori takes his head to his right to avoid the blow, and slides his right leg deeply between Uke's, and falls on his back.

Figure 27

The impetus of Uke's blow, and the fact that Tori has fallen out of the way, combined with Tori's lift with both hands, throws Uke over Tori's head to land with the rolling breakfall behind him. Uke lies where he has fallen for a moment, when both resume their feet, go to Tori's end of the kata, and repeat the throw in reverse.

3. Sumi Gaeshi

Tori advances until near enough to take hold. Both Tori and Uke assume a deep crouch, with feet widely spaced, knees bent. Each takes the normal hold on the sleeve with their left hand, but the right hand is thrust under the other's armpit to rest on the shoulder blade at the back.

Figure 28

Tori retreats two small steps, left-right. Uke follows right-left. They repeat this. On the third move, Tori does not retreat, but thrusts his left foot between Uke's legs, and raises his right, to place his instep against the inside of Uke's left knee. At the same time Tori falls on his back.

Figure 29

Now, with the impetus of his fall, a pull down with the hands and a lift on the inside of Uke's knee, Tori is able to throw Uke over his head. Uke does the right rolling breakfall down the mat. He remains lying down for a few seconds before both arise and go to the other end of the kata line, to repeat the movements on the opposite side.

This being the end of a set, they again go to their own ends of the kata line, adjust their jackets, then turn to face each other for the final set.

SET FIVE (Sacrifice Throws, falling on side)

1. Yoko Gake

This is another of the three-step throws. Tori approaches until near enough to take the normal holds. This time, however, Tori retreats with his right foot, followed by his left, the left dragging half a pace behind. Uke starts his advance with his right, stepping inside Uke's left foot, and following with his left, half a pace behind. As they make this advance, Tori turns Uke slightly to Uke's left, by pulling his right sleeve inwards.

Figure 30

On their second steps, which are like the first, Tori accentuates this turn. On the third step, Tori sweeps Uke's advancing right foot from behind the heel across his body, falls on his left side, and throws Uke by the pull down on his right sleeve. It is important however that Tori turns Uke onto his back, and does not bring him down onto his collar bone. He must support Uke with his left hand at the moment of falling.

Figure 31

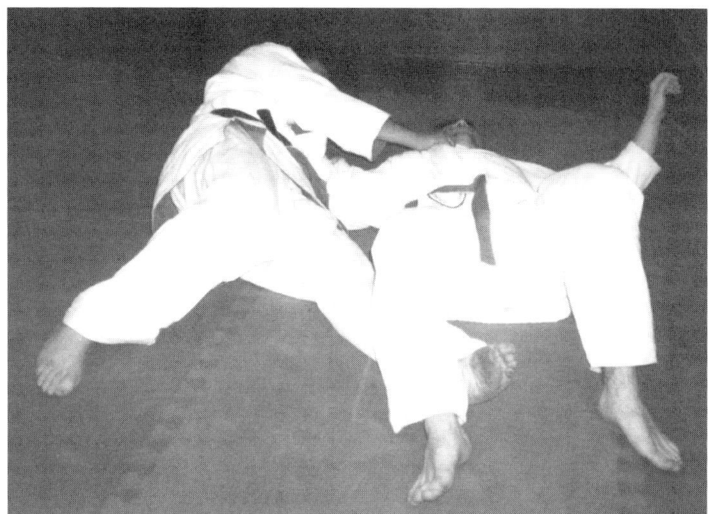

The throw is then repeated from the other end of the kata line, in reverse.

2. Yoko Guruma

The start is exactly the same as for Ura Nage, number 2 of the last set, but as Tori comes up to Uke, they both move to a position facing each other across the line of the kata, Uke with his back to the Joseki. Uke steps forward with his left, and attempts to strike the top of Tori's head as he brings his right foot forward. Tori moves in as before, putting his right hand in Uke's stomach, and his left on the belt behind. Uke bends forwards slightly to try and avoid Ura Nage. Tori inserts his right leg deeply between Uke's and swings around to fall on his left side at right angles to the axis of the kata, his head towards the Joseki. He is thus able to throw Uke directly down the line of the kata.

Figure 32

The throw is repeated from the opposite end, and in reverse.

3. Uke Waza

Like Sumi Gaeshi, this is a throw from a deep crouch. Tori approaches, and they take the holds as for Sumi Gaeshi and assume the deep crouch. Tori steps back, left-right.

Uke advances right-left. Tori again steps back left-right, and Uke follows right-left. On the third step, Tori stretches his left leg straight out, to block Uke's advance, and falls on his left side. Uke somersaults forwards with the rolling breakfall, directly down the line of the kata.

Figure 33

It is important that Tori lets Uke disengage his right arm to do the breakfall.
The throw is repeated in reverse from the other end.

Since this is the end of the kata, both Tori and Uke return to their original positions, and having adjusted their jackets, turn to face each other. They each step back, left right, to bring their heels together, and bow to each other. They then turn 45deg to face the joseki and bow to the guests, the standing bow being customary in each case.

Chapter 5

KATAME NO KATA

This kata again was created by Dr Jigoro Kano from his study of ancient movements. There are three sets of movements on the ground, and as with Nage No Kata every detail must be correct.

Tori and Uke take up positions twelve feet apart. Tori is to the right; and Uke to the left as viewed from the joseki. They stand perfectly still, silent and respectful for a few moments, before turning simultaneously to bow to the joseki. They then turn back to face each other, and step forward one pace, left-right so as to bring their feet normal distance apart. They then drop on their left knee, and turn their right knee outwards. This is known as the high kneeling position (Taka Kyoshi No Kamae). Note that the toes are dug into the mat. This is always so in a fighting position, and it is only when bowing that the toes are stretched out and the insteps are in contact with the mat.

Figure 34

From the high kneeling position, they simultaneously drop onto both knees, stretch out their toes, crossing their big toes, and make the kneeling bow.

See Figure 5, Chapter 1.

Having done this they return to the high kneeling position to begin the demonstration of groundwork. There are five movements in each set.

To get down onto his back, so that Tori may begin the demonstrations, Uke places both hands on the ground, and takes his right foot through, under his arms, so turning onto his back.

Figure 35

He lies along the axis of the kata, with his right leg extended and his left knee up, foot on floor.

Tori must remain in the high kneeling position while he does this. Now, before every movement, Tori must make an action known as "opening and closing the gate". As it is repeated often throughout the kata, one description only will be given here.

In the high kneeling position, left knee on the ground, Tori places his right palm on the inside of his right knee, and pushes it outwards, moving the leg and foot.

Figure 36

This is called "opening the gate", and signifies that an attack is about to be made. He must then place his right palm on the outside of his right knee, and push it back to the original position. This is called "closing the gate", and signifies that the attack is not real and in earnest, but is part of a friendly demonstration.

Before moving into the first demonstration, therefore, Tori will open and close the gate.

SET ONE (Holdings)

1. Kesa Gatame

Uke having lain down as described, Tori opens and closes the gate, arises to his feet, turns and walks three paces to his right, turns left and walks down to the right side of Uke, and takes up the high kneeling position. He now advances right leg first, bringing the left knee up, the two paces that brings him one pace away from Uke's right side. Here Tori opens and closes the gate. Whilst he is moving into this position, Tori should keep his eyes fixed on Uke, who should hold his head slightly off the mat. Tori now picks up Uke's right arm with his left hand holding the outer sleeve and his right hand holding the inner sleeve.

Figure 37

Tori puts Uke's right arm under his own left armpit, trapping it there, and drops onto Uke, by taking his right knee under Uke's right armpit, and his right arm under Uke's left armpit to hold his left shoulder to the ground. Tori is now in the scarf hold position, and relaxes on Uke.

Figure 38

Uke raises both his legs from the mat, swings them to right and to left, in an endeavour to unseat Tori, but when this fails, he taps Tori with his free left hand in token of submission.

Tori goes back to the high kneeling position at Uke's right side, ready for the second movement.

2. Kata Gatame

Tori opens and closes the gate. He then picks up Uke's right arm in his right, holding it by the wrist, and with his left hand pushes on the elbow to take it across Uke's throat.

Figure 39

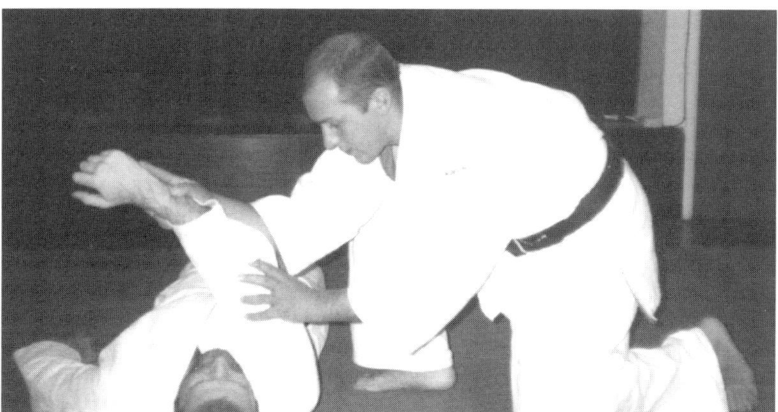

He then drops on Uke, taking his right knee under Uke's right armpit as before. At the same time he extends his left leg outwards. His right arm goes under Uke's neck, and he catches the hand in his left and pulls upwards. He lowers his head, thus trapping Uke's right upper arm against his neck. This is the Shoulder Hold.

Figure 40

Again, Uke raises both legs, swings them to right and to left, but fails to unseat Tori, and gives in by tapping. Tori returns to the high kneeling position.

3. Kami shiho gatame

Tori retreats three paces away from Uke, still on one knee, taking the knee back first and then the leg. At three paces, he arises, turns to his left, walks three paces, turns to his right, walks three paces, turns to face Uke and drops into the high kneeling position, looking down the line of the kata. He now advances on one knee starting with the right foot, until he is one pace away from Uke. He opens and closes the gate.

He now passes both hands under Uke's shoulders, and grasping Uke's belt on either side, pulls strongly to the ground. Tori lowers himself onto Uke, spreading both legs wide apart, and digging his toes into the mat. He places his right cheek on Uke's stomach, and relaxes all his weight on Uke.

Figure 41

Uke again tries to unseat him by raising his legs and swinging them from right to left, but without success. He submits by tapping.

Tori releases him, and taking the high kneeling position, retreats three paces on foot and knee. He then arises and comes to Uke's right side as before for the next movement.

4. Yoke Shiho Gatame

Tori is one pace away in the high kneeling position. He opens and closes the gate. He picks up Uke's left knee with his left hand, and putting his right arm between Uke's leg he grasps his belt at the back.

Figure 42

Tori now puts his left arm under Uke's head, and grasping his left shoulder holds it to the ground. Tori spreads his legs backwards and relaxes all his weight on Uke, digging his toes into the mat.

Figure 43

Uke again raises both his legs and tries by swinging them to left and to right to unseat Uke, but without avail. He submits by tapping. Tori releases him, takes the high kneeling position, and backs out on one knee three steps as before. He then arises and goes to his position behind Uke at the end of the kata line as at the end of kata gatame.

5. Kuzure Kami Shiho Gatame

Tori takes the high kneeling position, and comes in two paces, where he stops and opens and closes the gate. He then picks up Uke's right arm in his left hand, and traps it under his right armpit.

Figure 44

From here, he takes his left arm under Uke's left shoulder and catches his belt on his left hand side, pulling it to the ground. At the same time he lowers his body onto Uke, and spreads his legs, digging his toes into the mat.

Figure 45

Uke tries to escape as before, but without avail, and submits by tapping.

Tori releases him, takes the high kneeling position, and retreats on his knee and foot three paces to his own position at the end of the kata line.

Uke turns over, places both hands on the ground, and comes up to the high kneeling position by raising his right knee. They face each other and adjust their jackets, and there is a slight pause indicating the end of the first set. The important point about all these holdings is that Tori must relax on Uke, using all his weight to hold him, not stiffening up. If Tori is stiff, Uke will be able to move him. Think of Tori as a sack of fine flour. If one end were lifted, the flour would run to another part of the sack and all the weight would still be there. But if Tori is stiff, he is more like a box, with one end on the floor taking some of the weight, while Uke levers up an end.

SET TWO (Strangleholds)

Uke gets down onto his back as at the beginning of the first set. Tori arises and comes to his right side as before. One pace away he opens and closes the gate.

1. Kata Juji Jime

Tori picks up Uke's right arm in both his and lays it on the ground at right angles to his body. At the same time he slides his left knee in to make close contact with Uke's right side. He now swings his right leg across Uke, spreading Uke's left arm out at right angles to his body with his right hand as he does so. He now kneels astride Uke.

With his left hand he grasps Uke's left lapel, thumb inside and fingers outside, and applies the bony little finger edge of his forearm against Uke's throat. With his right hand he catches Uke's right lapel lower down, fingers inside and thumb out. By pulling down towards Uke's feet with the right hand and lowering the left elbow, Tori applies a stranglehold to Uke's throat.

Figure 46

Uke tries to sit forwards to relieve pressure, but Tori immediately throws his head forwards over Uke's right shoulder, thus increasing the pressure, so that Uke submits.

Tori comes back to the high kneeling position at Uke's right side, and retreats out on knee and foot three paces, then arises and returns to his starting position at the end of the kata line.

Uke sits up, with his left knee up and his right leg extended. Tori comes in three paces on his left knee to place himself behind Uke. He opens and closes the gate.

2. Ushiro Jime

Tori passes his right arm over Uke's right shoulder, and places the bony edge on the thumb side of the arm across the front of Uke's throat. He brings his right knee close behind Uke, pulling him back against this, which gives Uke support. Tori now takes his own right wrist in his left hand, palm uppermost, and pulls back towards himself, thus applying a naked stranglehold.

Figure 47

Uke submits by tapping.

It is permissible to vary this stranglehold by applying hadaka jime instead In this, instead of simply pulling the right wrist back with the left hand, the right palm is placed in the left elbow joint, and the left hand is applied to the back of Uke's head.

Figure 48

3. Okuri Eri Jime

Tori moves back one pace, and opens and closes the gate. Coming back in, to support Uke against his up-raised right knee, he uses his left hand to pull Uke's jacket loose on his left side. He then passes his right hand over Uke's right shoulder and across the front of his throat, to catch Uke's jacket well back behind his ear, thumb inside, on the left side.

Figure 49

Tori now puts his left hand under Uke's left and catches the right lapel of Uke's jacket. He pulls this down as he takes his right elbow back, thus applying the stranglehold. Uke catches his left sleeve with both hands to relieve pressure but it is useless.
Uke submits by tapping.

Tori releases him, moves back a pace, opens and closes the gate, and comes back in.

4. Kata Ha Jime

Tori moves in one pace and again uses his left hand to loosen Uke's jacket at the left side of his neck. Tori passes his right arm over Uke's right shoulder and across the front of his neck to take a hold high up on Uke's left collar, thumb inside. It is essential that the hold be far back behind Uke's ear as in the last movement. Tori now puts his left arm under Uke's left, as if to grasp his right lapel and to apply okuri eri (the last movement), but Uke foresees this and reaches up his left arm to try and seize Tori's head.

Tori immediately slides his left arm across the back of Uke's neck.

Figure 50

Uke catches Tori's left arm with both his and tries to pull down to release pressure, but it is useless, and he submits by tapping.

Tori releases him, and retreats the three Steps on his knee to his own end of the kata line. Uke lies down again, right leg extended, left knee up.

Tori comes to his right side as usual, and one pace away, he opens and closes the gate.

5. Gyaku Juji Jime

Tori picks up Uke's right arm in his hands and lays it at right angles to his body. He brings his left knee close against Uke's right side. He swings his right leg across, to kneel the other side, spreading Uke's left arm as he does so, so that this too is at right angles to his body. Tori is now kneeling astride Uke, knees close to his sides. He crosses his arms and catches Uke's collar on each side with fingers in and thumbs out. His hands should almost meet at the back of Uke's neck, and it is the bones on the thumb edge of his arms that press into Uke's neck.

Figure 51

Tori's right arm is over his left. Uke applies his left hand to Tori's right elbow and his right hand to Tori's left elbow, and suddenly he rolls to his left. Tori yields to this, going with Uke all the way, so that he is underneath and Uke is on top, but he has still retained the stranglehold. He now puts both his feet into Uke's body just below the hips, and lifts slightly. This applies the stranglehold even more vigorously, and Uke will submit.

Figure 52

They roll back to the original position. (Uke can help Tori to do this). Tori gets off Uke and takes the high kneeling position at his side, before retreating three paces on his knee, and returning to his place in the high kneeling position at his own end of the kata line. As this is the end of a set, Uke gets up to the high kneeling position as before, and they adjust their jackets. There is a slight pause.

SET THREE (Arm and Leg Locks)

Uke lies down again, and Tori comes to his right side in the same way as usual. One pace away he opens and closes the gate.

1. Ude Garami

Tori is in the High kneeling position. He moves in, after opening and closing the gate, so that his right shin is close to Uke's right side. Uke raises his left arm and tries to grab Tori's right lapel. With his left hand, Tori catches Uke's left wrist, and taking his right leg back, Tori falls across Uke's body, taking his left arm to the floor, in such a position that the upper arm is at right angles to his body, and the forearm is bent upwards and inwards towards his head. Tori puts his right arm under Uke's left and catches his own left wrist.

Figure 53

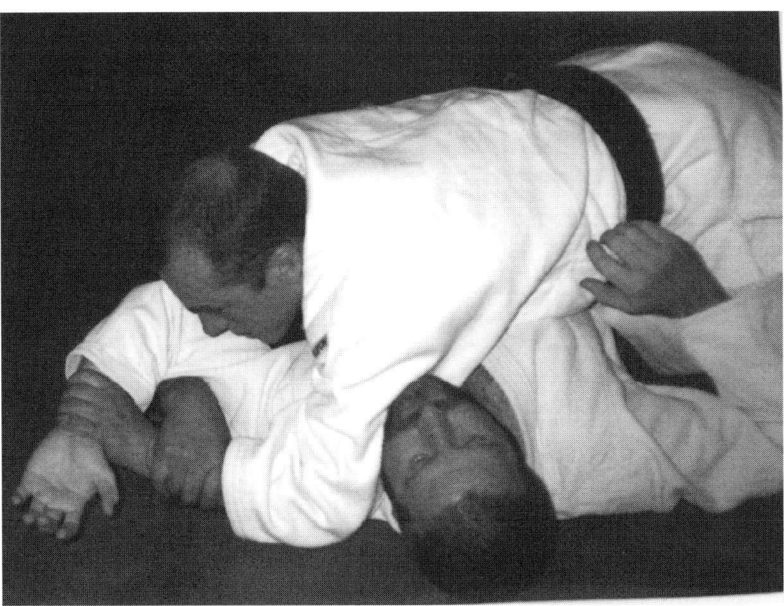

Now, by keeping his weight on Uke to prevent him sitting up, and by bending his own wrists to the ground, Tori will apply a painful bent armlock to Uke, who will submit.

Tori returns to the high kneeling position at Uke's right side. He again opens and closes the gate then moves in close.

2. Juji Gatame

This time, Uke raises his right arm to grasp Tori's left lapel. Tori catches his wrist with both hands, turning it so that Uke's elbow is towards him. At the same time he lifts his left leg over Uke's throat, and puts the foot on the ground on the other side of him. He now falls back, keeping his knees together to trap Uke's arm, and slightly raises his stomach, to apply pressure.

Figure 54

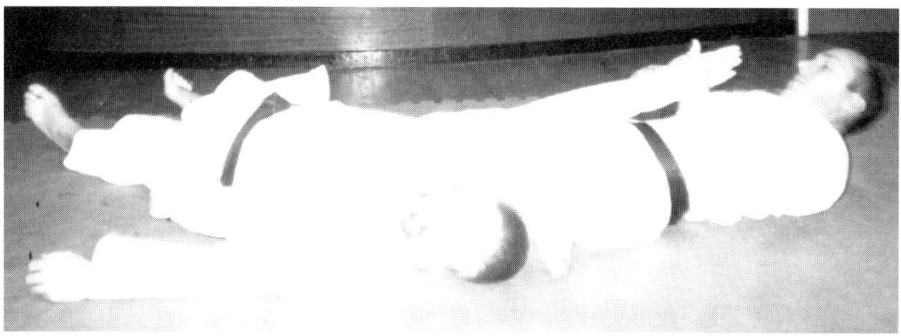

Uke submits. Tori returns to the high kneeling position, and opens and closes the gate. He then moves in close again, with his right shin against Uke's right side.

3. Ude Gatame

Uke reaches up with his left arm, turning slightly to his right as he does so, and tries to grasp Tori's right lapel.

Figure 55

Tori allows him to take the lapel hold, but clasping his hands over Uke's elbow, he imprisons it. With his right knee he kneels on Uke to prevent him moving away, and by bearing down on Uke's wrist with his right shoulder, and pulling Uke's elbow in towards himself, he applies the armlock. It is essential that Uke's elbow should be facing away from Tori.

Figure 56

Uke submits. Tori releases him and returns to the high kneeling position at his side. Tori now backs out as usual, and goes to his own end of the kata line, where he waits in the high kneeling position. Uke also gets up to the high kneeling position, and they approach each other on knee and foot until close enough to take the normal holds on sleeve and lapel.

4. Hiza Gatame

Tori lets go Uke's sleeve with his left hand, and by taking his arm over his wrist and his hand under Uke's arm he traps Uke's right arm under his left armpit.

Figure 57

Tori now places the sole of his right foot against Uke's left groin and pushing away takes Uke forwards and down. Tori turns to his right, brings his left knee up and uses it to press down on Uke's right elbow thus applying the knee armlock.

Figure 58

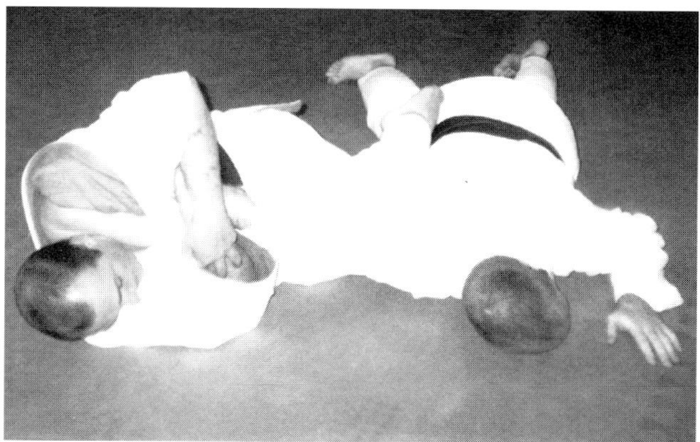

Uke submits by tapping. Both regain their feet.

5. Ashi Garami

Tori and Uke are standing normal distance apart, and they take the usual holds on each others sleeve and lapel. Uke takes a small step to his right with his right leg. Tori now slides his left foot well between Uke's legs, and raises his right leg as if he were going to attempt the tomoe nage throw described in Set four of Nage No Kata.

Figure 59

To avoid this, Uke steps well forward with his right foot, bringing it forward as far as Tori's armpit.

Tori now abandons tomoe nage, and wraps his left leg around Uke's right from the outside, retaining his holds on Uke's jacket, and bringing him forwards. He pushes with his right foot against Uke's left shin, so spreading his legs, and this applies a painful leglock to Uke's right knee.

Figure 60

Uke gives in by tapping.

It should be pointed out that leglocks are banned in judo, and this one is never seen outside the kata, so is not described elsewhere in this book.

They resume their standing position, go to their own ends of the kata line, and as this is the end of the demonstration they adjust their jackets.

They take the high kneeling position together, drop into position for the kneeling bow to each other, then arise to make the standing bow to the joseki.

Chapter 6

KAESHI KATA

There are several katas showing throws and counter-throws, most of them of more modern origin than the earlier katas. Kaeshi kata is considered by many to most truly reflect the principles of judo, and consists of nine throws and nine counter-movements.

The performers stand on the axis of the kata, Tori to the right Uke to the left, as viewed from the joseki. They turn towards the joseki together and make the standing bow, then turn to face each other and make the standing bow to each other. They then each step forwards one pace, left foot then right, to bring their feet normal distance apart, since their heels were together when bowing.

They approach to normal distance apart, so that they can each take the usual holds on each other's jacket lapel and sleeve, and they are then ready to begin the demonstration.

1. De Ashi Barai countered by De Ashi Barai

The first movement is de ashi barai, sweeping an advancing foot. Tori advances his right foot slowly, keeping the sole close to the ground and stepping directly forward. This is a step that would be avoided if possible in judo contest, since it gives the perfect opportunity for de ashi barai. Uke pulls down on Tori's right sleeve with his left hand and lifts with his right, so as to accentuate Tori's displacement to his right. At the same time, with the sole of his left foot, Uke sweeps Tori's advancing right foot across his body. The moment for applying the sweep is just as Tori is transferring the weight onto his right foot.

Figure 61

This throw by Uke on Tori is performed slowly, so that the audience may see what throw is being attempted when the counter is done. It is important that it be done accurately, in the best possible style, since katas are intended to enshrine the most perfect movements for future students.

Tori is thrown. He gets up with the minimum of movement and now advances his right foot the second time, giving Uke the same opportunity for the throw. This time, however, when Uke attempts to throw him, he steps over Uke's attempted foot sweep, and sweeps his advancing left foot instead, pulling down on his left lapel and lifting his right elbow, so as to displace Uke to his left side. Uke is thus thrown with the same throw de ashi barai.

Figure 62

2. 0 Uchi Gari countered by Ushiro Goshi

The second throw is O Uchi Gari, the major inner reaping throw. Tori stands with his feet somewhat wider apart, to facilitate this throw, which is usually attempted on a person who adopts that stance and pulls you around the mat. Uke steps in with his left foot, pointing it across Tori's body to his right. At the same time he pins Tori on his heels, by pushing down on Tori's right sleeve towards Tori's right heel, and pushing over Tori's left shoulder and down to his left heel with the right hand. Uke now uses his right leg to reap Tori's left leg away with a hooking movement from the inside.

Figure 63

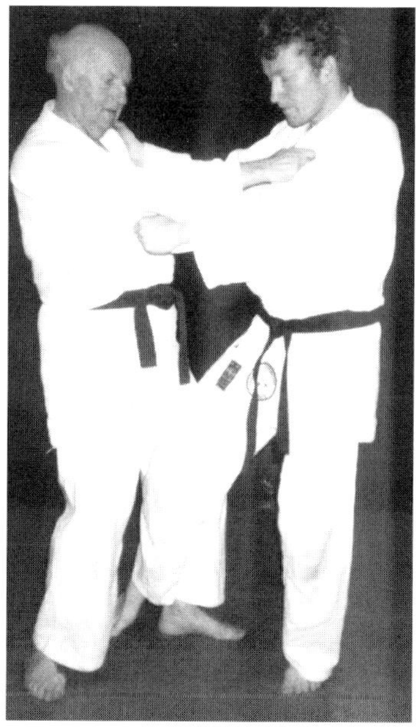

The direction of the reap is circular, Uke's toes describing an are backwards in a quarter circle. Ideally his toes should brush the mat when doing this. Tori is thrown, and when he gets up, Uke attempts the same throw on him at normal speed.

Tori bends his knees to lower his body, grasps Uke round the waist with both hands, right in front, left behind, and throws his stomach forwards to lift Uke clear of the ground. He may help this movement by raising his left knee if he wishes. Uke is lifted clear and can be dropped directly onto his back in front of Tori.

Figure 64

3. Ko Uchi Gari countered by Hiza Guruma

Uke takes his left foot back in a small quarter circle, to turn his right side to Tori. At the same time he pulls gently on Tori's right sleeve, level with the ground, to make him take a step forwards with his right foot. At the moment he does this, Uke places the sole of his right foot behind Tori's right heel and sweeps it forwards in the direction it is going. Ideally, both Tori's foot and Uke's must be as near the ground as possible. The right side of Uke's right foot, would be brushing the mat, as Tori would be sliding his foot forward in close contact with the mat.

Figure 65

The effect of this throw is like stepping on a banana skin. The right foot shoots forward a little farther than intended and Tori falls flat on his back.

Although it is difficult to perform these sweeping throws slowly, an attempt should be made to slow them down enough for the audience to see what happens.

Uke now attempts the throw at normal speed. Tori foresees his attempt, and swivelling towards Uke on his left foot, he places his right sole on the outside of Uke's left knee. Since Uke is standing on that leg, his right foot being off the ground for throwing purposes, he can easily be unbalanced, by Tori turning to his own right and pulling round and down with his right hand and lifting with his left. The throw is hiza guruma.

Figure 66

4. 0 Goshi countered by Utsuri Goshi

0 goshi is the major hip throw. Uke steps in with his right foot to just inside Tori's right foot, turning his body as he goes to bring his back to Tori, and taking his left foot to just inside Tori's left foot. Uke's right hand goes around Tori's back to rest on his right shoulder blade, and with his left he pulls Tori onto him. By going in with knees slightly bent and straightening them he can thus take Tori onto his right hip, for the major hip throw.

Figure 67

He throws Tori in front of him. Tori arises, and Uke attempts the same throw at normal speed.

As Uke comes in, Tori bends his knees and grasps him around the waist with both hands, right in front and left behind. Throwing his stomach forwards he is able to lift Uke clear of the ground, and swinging Uke's legs backwards, he is able to insert his own left hip under Uke and to do a hip throw on the opposite side.

Figure 68

This is known as the changing hip throw.

5. Harai Goshi countered by Ushiro Goshi

Uke moves in for a hip throw as described in 4, but when he is in position, he takes his weight entirely on his left leg, and raises his right to sweep the outside of Tori's right thigh, so increasing the effectiveness of the throw by sweeping his legs from under him.

Figure 69

Tori is thrown in front of Uke. He gets up, and Uke attempts the same throw again.

Tori bends his knees to lower his centre of gravity, seizes Uke round the waist with both arms, right in front, and throwing his stomach forward as before, he is able to lift Uke clear of the ground, when he straightens his legs. He may assist this by lifting with his right knee if he wishes.

Figure 70

Tori can now drop Uke in front of him with the throw known as Ushiro Goshi.

6. Hani Goshi countered by Tsurikomi Ashi

Uki moves in for a hip throw similarly to the way described above, but this time his right side is to Tori rather than his back, and he lifts his right leg bent at the knee and places it across the front of Tori's legs. His right side and his bent leg together form a kind of table on which Tori's body rests, as Uke leans away to take him off his feet.

Figure 71

By straightening his left leg on which he is standing and turning, Uke can throw Tori to the ground in front of him with the spring hip throw.

Tori arises, and Uke comes in for the same throw again. His weakness is that he is standing on one leg only. Tori places the sole of his right foot against the left shinbone of Uke, and by turning to his own right, and the use of a pull with his right hand, he is able to throw Uke over this leg with the Drawing Ankle throw.

Figure 72

7.0 Soto Gari countered by Harai Goshi

Uki moves in to Tori's right side, placing his left foot on a line drawn through Tori's feet, and just outside his right foot. Uke pushes down with his left hand towards Tori's right heel, thus pinning him on that heel. With his right hand he pushes up and over Tori's left shoulder and down towards his left heel. Tori is thus pinned on his heels. When doing this Uke must take his whole body in, so that it is his whole body weight pressing against Tori that pins him. He looks over Tori's right shoulder at the spot where Tori will fall. He now brings his right leg through between his own left and Tori's right, and swinging it forward, uses the return swing to sweep Tori's right leg from under him.

Figure 73

Tori falls on his back. He gets up, and Uke attempts the same throw again. This time, as Uke attempts to pin him, Tori quickly spins around with his back to Uke , by withdrawing his left foot and turning on his right. He slides his right arm round Uke's waist, and with his left pulls Uke onto him for a hip throw. Raising his right leg, he sweeps Uke's legs from the outside with the sweeping hip throw.

Figure 74

8. 0 Uchi Mata countered by Uki Otoshi

Uke brings Tori onto his toes with a pull forwards, and turns in by taking his left foot back and around in a small circle that brings his left foot just outside Tori's left, and pointing the same way. Uke inserts his right leg between Tori's, so as to sweep his left thigh from the inside.

Figure 75

By continuing the turn, combined with the sweep, Uki is able to throw Tori with the inner thigh throw.

Tori falls on his back. He gets up, and Uke again tries the same movement. His weakness is that when he lifts his right leg to throw, he is standing on one leg. Tori takes his own left leg back out of reach, whilst resisting the pull forward that would unbalance him. He then transfers his weight onto his left leg, and turns by taking his right foot back in a small circle around his left. By pulling down with his right hand and lifting with his left, in the action of turning a steering wheel, he is able to throw Uke in the hand throw.

Figure 76

9. Ippon Seoi Nage countered by Uki Waza

Uke turns in as for a hip throw, but this time, instead of putting his right arm round Tori's back, he thrusts it under Tori's right armpit, and by straightening his legs is able to lift Tori onto his back for the shoulder throw.

Figure 77

He now has only to continue turning, to throw Tori over his shoulder to the ground in front of him. Tori gets up, and Uke again attempts the same throw.

This time, as Tori is lifted from the ground, he places his right palm against Uke's right hip to push him away, swings his body right round in front of Uke, and falls on his back. With his right hand he lifts under Uke's left armpit, and by rolling onto his left side is able to throw Uke with a sacrifice throw.

Figure 78

Uke does the rolling breakfall, and comes to his feet. Tori gets up.

As this is the end of the demonstration, both retire to their own ends of the kata line, and turning their backs to each other, they adjust their jackets.

They then turn to face each other, step back, left right to bring their heels together, and make the formal bow to each other. They then turn towards the joseki and bow to the guests or master seated there.

Some Judo organisations prefer GONOSEN NO KATA to be demonstrated instead of Kaeshi kata. This is a series of throws and counter-throws, and was created by masters of the Waseda University in Japan about fifty years ago. It is performed in exactly the same way, except that there is a different sequence of throws and counters. Students who are familiar with the throws will have no difficulty in working out what to do from the following table:

1. 0 soto gari is countered by 0 soto gari.
2. Hiza Guruma is countered by Hiza Guruma.
3. 0 Uchi Gari is countered by De Ashi Barai.
4. De Ashi Barai is countered by De Ashi Barai.
5. Ko Soto Gake is countered by Tai Otoshi.
6. Ko Uchi Gari is countered by Tsurikomi Ashi.
7. Kube Nage is countered by Ushiro Goshi.
8. Koshi Guruma is countered by Uki Goshi.
9. Hane Goshi is countered by Tsurikomi Ashi.
10. Harai Goshi is countered by Utsuri Goshi.
11. Uchi Mata is countered by Sukui Nage.
12. Kata Seoi is countered by Sumi Gaeshi.

Some of the counters are the same as in Kaeshi Kata, others different. The student will work out which he prefers. Certainly, the practice of either Kaeshi kata or Gonosen No Kata will be invaluable to contest orientated students, as frequent practice of these katas will make countering almost automatic.

Chapter 7

JU NO KATA

The three katas already described cover the basic grammar of judo in terms of throws, counter-throws and groundwork techniques. Ju No Kata is the kata of suppleness. It was considered of great importance by Professor Kano, who insisted that it should be practised frequently.

It is both a physical exercise and a means of practising basic movements correctly. For example, many of the evasions of attack are made by the simple turning movement (tai sabaki) described in the first section of this book. It needs practice to perform these seemingly-simple movements correctly, and Ju No Kata is an interesting way of getting that practice.

Ju No Kata does not require strength to perform, nor does it need judo clothing, though it is usually done in such. It does not need a mat since there are no throws, so it can in fact be performed anywhere, simply as a physical exercise. In formal demonstrations, it is often performed by women, but not necessarily so. Today, the kata is always performed slowly, though in former times, it was sometimes done at normal speeds. It is important, however, that the attacks made in the kata should be real. The person attacked must be forced to take the avoiding action, otherwise the kata is false and has no meaning.

There are three sets of five movements, but often today they are done as a continuous series of fifteen without breaks. I have indicated the breaks; it is for each master to decide whether he prefers it with or without them.

Tori and Uke stand on the kata line about twelve feet apart, as usual, Tori to the right, Uke to the left, as seen from the Joseki.

They turn towards the joseki and bow as usual, then turn to face each other and bow to each other, both bows in the standing position. They then step forwards, left-right, to bring their feet normal distance apart, since the bow was made with heels together.

1. Tsuki Dashi

Uke advances towards Tori, right foot first, left trailing, and as he does so, he raises his right hand, arm straight and fingers stiff. Three steps should bring him close enough to stab Uke between the eyes with his fingers, but he raises his arm slightly higher on each of the three steps.

Figure 79

As he reaches Tori, Tori must avoid the stab by Tai Sabaki, taking her right foot back and her body parallel to the line of thrust. As she does so she seizes Uke's right wrist in her's, fingers uppermost, and pulls Uke, forcing him to take the extra step, which brings him immediately in front of Tori. Tori now takes Uke's left wrist in her left hand, fingers down, thumb uppermost, and stretches his arms out, the right up and the left downwards.

Figure 80

Tori now leans back slightly, stretching Uke's spine backwards. Uke bends his knees slightly, and turning to his left, he makes a complete about turn, reversing the hold on Tori, and stretching her backwards.

Figure 81

Tori bends her knees slightly and reverses the hold again, by continuing to turn in the same direction. This brings her back to the position in Figure 80. As it is obvious that Uke could turn again and the reversal of positions could continue indefinitely, Tori now places her left hand on Uke's left shoulder, raises Uke's right arm above his head, and takes a step back, left-right, so as to bend Uke backwards.

Figure 82

Uke is clearly unbalanced. If Tori went any farther Uke would fall on his back. Also Uke's spine is being bent backwards, which could be injurious. He signifies his submission by tapping his thigh with his left hand, and Tori takes him back to the upright position, and lowers his right arm to his side.

This concern for Uke, in placing his arm in its proper place each time is one of the features of the kata, and should not be omitted.

2. Kata Oshi.

Tori now takes one full pace to her left with her left foot, and turns to face away from Uke, by bringing her right foot forward one pace. She is thus astride the line of the kata, with her back to Uke. Uke takes his left foot back, making a quarter turn, which brings him to face Tori's back, a pace behind her, and with his right foot midway between Tori's. Uke now pushes Tori's right shoulder with the palm of his right hand.

Tori bends forwards so that the palm slides over her shoulder, and reaching up with her right hand, she catches Uke's right, so that her thumb is in the palm and her fingers on the back.

Figure 83

Tori now backs under Uke's right arm to stand on the kata line facing Uke's back, and lifting Uke's right wrist. This causes such a painful lock on the wrist, that Uke will turn to avoid it, and attempt to strike Tori between the eyes with his left hand, palm uppermost.

Figure 84

Tori, however, catches Uke's left hand, thumb in palm in the same hold that she has on Uke's right, and turns Uke completely, so that Uke has his back to Tori. Tori now raises Uke's arms above his head, and bends him backwards by pulling on them, thus causing possible danger to the spine.

Figure 85

Uke will submit by tapping the floor with his left foot.

3. Ryote Dori

Tori will return Uke to the upright, and will place Uke's arms back by his sides. Whilst Uke stands still, Tori will walk round to stand in front of him, facing Uke and one pace away.

Uke leans forwards and grabs Tori's wrists, the right in his left, the left in his right, thumbs inside. It is important that Tori does not present her wrists to Uke, but makes Uke reach forward to grab them, thus putting Uke off balance.

Figure 86

Tori takes her right foot forward, disengaging her right wrist, and turning her back to Uke by taking her right foot through. She takes her right arm over Uke's right, trapping it under her right armpit.

Figure 87

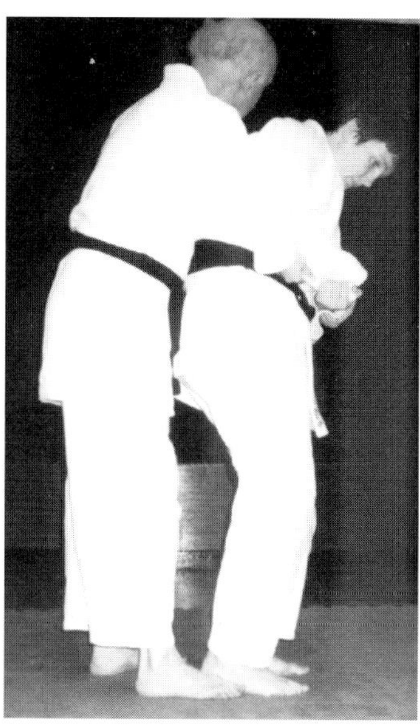

Tori now bends forward, thus lifting Uke from the ground, as if she would throw him with the sacrifice throw known as makikomi, but she does not complete the throw. She simply lifts Uke clear of the ground.

Uke, for his part, maintains his body stiff, and raises his legs high in the air, balancing on Tori's body, by placing his left hand on the back of Tori's left hip.

Figure 88

They hold the position for a moment, after which Tori lowers Uke to the ground again. Tori is now standing with her back to Uke and in front of him.

4. Kata Mawashi

Uke now places the palm of his left hand on the top of Tori's left shoulder, and with the palm of his right hand he presses the back of Tori's right shoulder-blade, so as to turn her around.

Figure 89

Tori yields to the push, and turns by taking her right foot forward and around in a complete circle. At the same time, she takes her right arm over Uke's left, down, and up under Uke's right, so that her own right shoulder is under Uke's armpit.

Figure 90

She is now in a position to do the shoulder throw, Seoi Nage, but she simply lifts Uke onto her back, without completing the throw. Uke, for his part, raises his legs high, keeping his body stiff. They hold the pose for a moment, before Tori lowers Uke to the ground again.

Figure 91

5. Age Oshi

Tori now walks several paces forwards, and turns to face away from the joseki. Uke advances with tsugi ashi, beginning with his right foot, and raising his right arm stiffly, fingers together, to stab Tori in the chin. Unlike the first movement, Uke does not raise his arm higher with each step, but takes it straight up to the position before taking the first step.

As he gets near enough to strike, Tori must take her head back so that the thrust passes harmlessly by. She must then catch Uke's right hand, thumb in palm, fingers at back, in her right hand.

Figure 92

Tori now backs under Uke's raised right arm, and backs down the line of the kata. This, as in movement 2, puts such a painful lock on Uke's wrist, that he will turn to face Tori and attempt to strike her between the eyes with his left hand, fingers stiff and palm uppermost.

Figure 93

Again, Tori will catch his hand with the same hold as the other, thumb in palm, and will completely turn Uke, so that Uke has his back to her, raising his arms above his head.

Figure 94

To counter this, Uke will try bending his arms, but the wrist locks are still effective, and Tori steps back a pace to increase the effect, and bend his spine. Uke surrenders by tapping the ground with his left heel as before.

This is the end of the first set of five, and if a pause it being made here, both Tori and Uke will retire to their respective ends of the kata line, and will turn their backs on each other to adjust their jackets. They will then turn to face each other again, ready for the second set.

6. Kiri Oroshi

For the first movement of the second set, Uke turns to face the joseki, and slowly raises his right arm fingers extended, as he breathes in deeply. He now turns to face Tori, and coming towards her, he strikes down at her head with the little finger edge of his right hand, using it as if it were a blade to cleave Tori down through the middle.

Figure 95

Tori takes back her head, so that the blow comes down in front of her, and as Uke's arm descends, she catches it by the wrist in her right hand. She will step back a little to avoid the blow. Having seized Uke's wrist, she advances with the Tsugi Ashi movement, beginning with her right foot, two paces.

Figure 96

Uke is forced to move with her, but he takes a third pace so as to free his right arm, and with his left hand he pushes on Tori's elbow to turn her away.

Figure 97

Tori yields to this push, and as she ducks under Uke's left arm, she catches Uke's left hand with her own left hand, thumb in palm and fingers at the back. In making this turn she must spin on her left foot without moving it.

Figure 98

This brings her behind Uke, to Uke's left side. She places her right hand on Uke's left shoulder, and raises Uke's left arm above his head, still with the hold on his hand. She retreats a step to take Uke off balance backwards, and Uke submits to the spine lock.

Figure 99

7. Ryo Kata Oshi

Tori now comes to stand in front of Uke facing down the line of the kata with her back to him. Uke raises both hands and presses down on Tori's shoulders.

Figure 100

Tori bends her knees deeply, turns around, and seizes Uke's right wrist with both hands. She then advances with three quick little steps, pulling Uke behind her with the hold on his wrist. To prevent this, Uke places his left hand against Tori's left hip.

Figure 101

Reacting to this, Tori takes her left foot behind Uke, her left arm across Uke's chest, and raises Uke's right arm in the air. Now, by turning slightly to her own left, Tori can inflict a spine lock on Uke, who submits.

Figure 102

8. Naname Uchi.

Tori and Uke are at their respective ends of the kata line. Uke advances, and bending his right arm across his chest, he strikes Uke with the little finger edge of his right hand. Tori dodges by bending backwards and Uke's hand passes in front of her face.

Figure 103

Tori now attacks Uke, by stabbing at his eyes with the fingers of her right hand. Uke dodges this by a quarter turn (Tai Sabaki) to his left, taking his left foot back. Uke seizes Tori's right wrist in his left hand.

Figure 104

Tori now catches Uke's left wrist with her left hand. Uke pushes on her left elbow with his right, so turning Tori , who comes to Uke's left side. Tori bends her knees, catches Uke around the waist, and lifts him clear of the ground, so that she could throw him by falling. She does not complete the throw, however, and Uke submits by clapping his hands together above his head.

Figure 105

9. Katate Dori

Tori now comes to stand on Uke's right side, both on the line of the kata. Uke takes Tori's left wrist in his right hand. To escape from this, Tori takes her left arm across her body.

Figure 106

Uke now pushes Tori's left shoulder with his left arm turning Tori more, so that she can slip under Uke for a Hip Throw.

Figure 107

She does not complete the throw of course, but puts Uke back on his feet.

10. Katate Age

Both go to their respective ends of the kata line. They raise their right arms above their heads, and come towards each other with short rapid steps on their toes. They meet, their right arms locking at the shoulders.

Figure 108

To avoid this, Tori takes her right foot back, with the quarter turn (Tai Sabaki). This leads Uke's right arm to descend with its own momentum. Tori catches Uke's right wrist and takes it down further, making Uke bend to his right.

Figure l09

Uke resists this, straightens up, and by pulling down on his left arm and lifting under his right armpit, Tori makes him bend over to his left. Uke resists this, and comes upright again, and since this reversal could go on, Tori stops it, by placing her left hand on Uke's left shoulder, and raising Uke's right arm, held at the wrist, high in the air, and stepping back. Uke is now off balance backwards, and could be made to fall or have his spine painfully bent, so he submits by tapping his thigh with his left hand.

Figure 110

This again being the end of a set, they go to their own ends of the kata line, adjust their jackets, and turn to face each other for the final set.

11. Obi Tori

Uke crosses his right arm over his left, and advances with the intention of seizing Tori's belt. Tori catches Uke's right arm, which is uppermost, with her own palms turned upwards, her left hand seizing Uke's wrist from underneath, and her right seizing Uke's elbow.

Figure 111

Tori now pushes on Uke's elbow to turn him about, and as his back comes towards Tori, she uses her left hand on Uke's left shoulder to help pull him around.

Figure 112

As Uke completes his turn, he pushes on Tori's left elbow with his right hand, so turning Tori away from him. Tori slides her right arm round Uke's waist, and picks him up for a hip throw.

Figure 113

She does not complete the throw of course, but puts Uke down, and they stand facing each other, ready for the next movement.

12. Muni Oshi

Uke approaches Tori and with his right hand, palm flat, pushes Tori's left chest. Tori pushes Uke's left chest in the same way with her right hand. Both Tori and Uke grasp the other's wrist, fingers outside, thumbs in, and raise the hands above the head.

Figure 114

Uke now takes the initiative, and bending his fingers around Tori's wrist, he brings his right arm down, at the same time turning to his left in an anti-clockwise movement. Tori follows, turning to her right in a clockwise movement , and letting her fingers slide round Uke's wrist.

Figure 115

They continue the rotation. At the moment when they have turned a full circle, Tori has Uke's left arm in the air, and she slides her fingers down to grasp it at the elbow. She has Uke's right wrist, held down. She now steps behind Uke with her right foot, and slightly turning to her left applies a twisting spine lock on Uke.

Figure 116

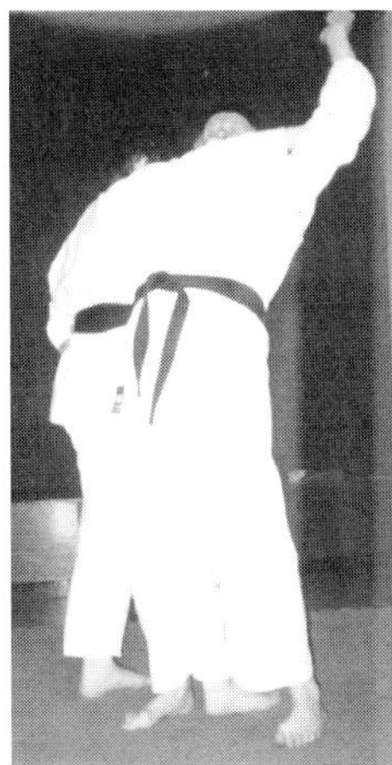

Uke submits by tapping with his left foot.

13. Tsuki Age

Uke steps back a pace with his right foot, and clenches his right fist. He then steps forward with his right foot to deliver a right uppercut to Tori's jaw. Tori bends back slightly so that the blow passes her jaw harmlessly. She then cups her right hand over Uke's right fist, and by a push on his right elbow with her open left hand, she turns Uke away.

Figure 117

Uke immediately yields to this, and pivots a full circle, to again attempt the uppercut. Tori cups her hand over his fist as before, but this time she steps in with her right foot, puts her left arm behind Uke's right, and bends Uke's right arm back in an armlock, similar to Ude Garami in the Katame No Kata.

Figure 118

14. Uchi Oroshi

Uke comes to within a pace of Tori. Clenching his right fist, he takes it in a clockwise circle in front of him, and then raises it to make a strike on the top of Tori's skull with the bottom of his fist. Tori leans back to dodge the blow, or may retreat with small steps to do so.

Figure 119

She catches Uke's right wrist in her right as it passes harmlessly down and stepping forward with her right foot. Tori forces Uke to retreat with his right. After two steps with each foot, Uke takes the third step, as in Number 6, so as to release his arm. He then pushes on Tori's right elbow with his left to push her away.

Figure 120

Again, as in Number 6, Tori turns, ducking under Uke's arm to come behind him. As she does so, she catches Uke's left hand with her own left, thumb in palm, fingers at back. It is important when making this turn that she does not move her left foot, but spins on it, until she is behind Uke. She can then move it back.

Figure 121

When behind Uke, she brings Uke's left arm across her stomach to do the stomach armlock, and puts her right arm round Uke's neck to apply a stranglehold.

Figure 122

Uke submits and they go to their own ends of the kata line.

15. Ryogan Tsuki

Uke advances on Tori and raises his right arm with the fingers divided in a "V", and attempts to strike Tori in the eyes with the finger tips.

Figure 123

Tori blocks this from the inside with her raised left arm. Uke now catches Tori's left wrist with his left hand, turning slightly to his right as he does so.

Figure 124

Tori pushes on Uke's left elbow with her right hand so as to turn him around completely. Uke will duck his head under Tori's right arm. As Uke comes to face her again, Tori attempts to stab Uke in the eyes with her left hand, fingers open in the "V".

Figure 125

Uke blocks this from the inside with his right, and Tori grabs his right wrist with her right hand.

Figure 126

Uke now pushes on Tori's right elbow with his left hand, so as to turn her. Tori slides her left arm round Uke's waist, so that she is in a position to do the Hip Throw (0 goshi) on the left side.

Figure 127

Although she picks Uke up, she does not complete the throw, but puts Uke back on his feet. As this is the end of the kata, they return to their respective ends, and adjust their jackets, preliminary to making the standing bow to each other, and then to the joseki.

Chapter 8

KIME NO KATA

Kime No Kata is a kata of self-defence. It is normally required as part of the examination for progress through the Dan grades. There are two parts. The first set of movements is performed kneeling and consists of eight attacks and eight counters. This kneeling position may look artificial to Western eyes, but it would be the normal seated posture in a Japanese household in the older days when people did not sit on chairs but on cushions laid on the floor. Practice of movement from this position will strengthen the ankle joints and knees making them more supple. The second set of movements consists of twelve attacks and counters in a standing position.

Some of the attacks use the sword, which is the long Samurai two-handed sword. Others use the dagger, a short and more personal weapon. Before practising with either, the student should become proficient at evasion with imitation weapons, since the real ones are razor sharp, and the attacks must be real. The kata should not be faked.

When they come onto the mat, Tori is on the right and Uke on the left as viewed from the joseki. Uke carries the weapons in his right hand, with the curvature upwards. The dagger is held closest to his body; the sword on the outside. At a distance of twelve feet from each other, they pause, and ceremoniously make the standing bow to the joseki.

They now take the high kneeling position, described in Katame No Kata left knee on the ground. Uke lays down his weapons on his right side. The curvature of the sword is towards himself, the dagger is nearest to him, and the hilt of the sword is in line with his right foot.

They now both drop onto both knees, and with big toes crossed behind them, they make the kneeling bow to each other.

Figure 128

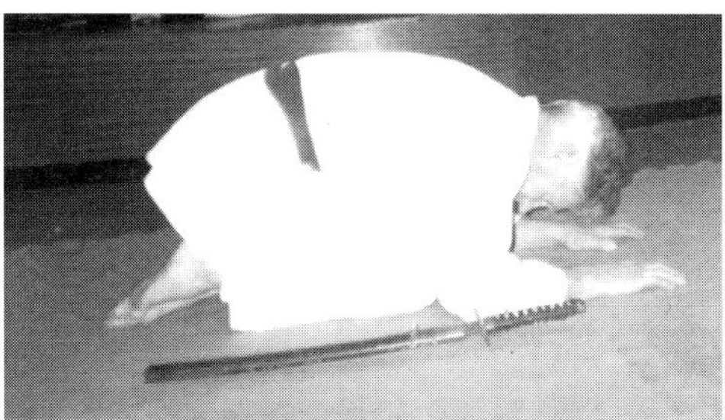

They come back to the high kneeling position, Uke picks up his weapons, placing them in his left hand, one by one, then transferring them back to his right, curvature still upwards, and dagger inside. Whilst Tori still remains in the high kneeling position, Uke arises, turns about, goes to the end of the kata line, kneels, first in the high kneeling position and then on both knees, and lays down his weapons. When doing this his insteps must be facing towards the mat, as when bowing. His toes are only dug in when making an attack.

He places the weapons with the dagger nearest to him, and the hilts pointing towards the joseki, the points away from it. The weapons are thus at right angles to the line of the kata, and the curvature is towards Uke.

Uke now arises and approaching Tori, he takes the high kneeling position a few paces away. They both drop onto their knees, and place their fists on the ground with the thumbs pointing towards each other.

Figure 129

Their toes are still extended. They are only dug into the mat at the moment of attack. They approach on their hands and knees until they are about six inches apart, and are then ready for the first attack.

SET ONE (Attacks kneeling)

1. Ryote Dori

Uke rises on his toes, toes dug into mat, and seizes Uke's wrists, right in his left hand, left in his right hand.

Figure 130

Tori also rises on his toes, toes dug into mat. He parts his arms slightly, so as to unbalance Uke forwards, and with his right foot delivers a kick to Uke's abdomen. Care should be taken not to land this, or any of the blows described, but to stop just short, of course.

Figure 131

The kick is accompanied by a shout emanating from the lower abdomen, called a kiai. It is really a sharp expulsion of breath, concentrating the force of the counter-attack, rather as karate men shout when they strike. Although, we shall not repeat the instruction, this shout accompanies each counter attack in the kata.

Having delivered the kick, Tori replaces his right knee on the ground, and opening his right hand, he lifts Uke's left, so as to grasp his wrist, whilst turning to his own left. Taking his left foot back around, parallel to the line of the kata, he raises his left knee, and holding Uke's wrist with both hands, is able to apply an armlock to his left elbow.

Figure 132

Uke taps in submission. They return to the kneeling position feet extended, about a foot apart. For many of the attacks which follow, either with fist, dagger, or sword, it is necessary to clearly visualise the axis of the kata, that is an imaginary line drawn through the centre of the participants. Any punch or stab or cut is made directly along this line, and Tori's first move must always be to take the whole of his body behind the line so that the blow or stab or cut will pass harmlessly in front of him. Self-preservation is the first step in self defence; counter movements follow.

2. Tsuki Kake

Uke comes up onto his toes, and aims a direct right-hand punch at Tori's solar plexus. Tori raises his hips, digs his toes into the mat, and pivots on his left knee, so that the blow will pass in front of him. He must take his body over the line of the kata, out of the way. At the same time, he catches Uke's right elbow with his left hand, and pulls him forward, to deliver a blow between his eyes with the right fist. Be careful not to land the blow of course, as you are pulling him onto it.

Figure 133

Tori now changes hands, and catches Uke's right wrist in his right hand, and takes his left hand over Uke's left shoulder to grasp his right lapel. By thrusting his stomach forward against Uke's right elbow, and pulling back with his right hand, he applies a straight armlock to Uke's right arm and with his left, he is applying a stranglehold to Uke's throat.

Figure 134

Uke submits by tapping and they return to facing each other.

3. Suri Age

Uke rises on his toes, toes dug into the mat, and with the heel of his right hand tries to strike a blow at Tori's forehead.

Figure 135

Tori bends slightly backwards so that the blow passes harmlessly upwards, and coming up onto his toes, he wards off the blow, by catching Uke's wrist with his right hand, and applying his left palm to Uke's right shoulder. As he does this he delivers a kick with his right foot to Uke's abdomen.

Figure 136

This brings Uke forward. Tori replaces his right knee on the ground, and takes Uke down onto his face. He now advances on his knees towards Uke's outstretched right arm, left, right, left, and on the second left, he kneels with his left knee on Uke's right elbow. This applies a painful armlock, if Tori lifts Uke's right wrist, and Uke will submit.

Figure 137

They return to the normal position facing each other.

4. Yoko Uchi.
Uki rises on his toes, and with his right fist aims a blow at Tori's left temple. This is one of the atemi-waza strikes, made with the bottom of the fist.

Figure 138

Tori dodges the blow, raises his right knee close to Uke's right side, and with his right hand pushes Uke's left shoulder back. His own right shoulder close against Uke's arm prevents him drawing it away for a second blow.

Figure 139

Tori places his left hand in Uke's back, and is thus able to force him over backwards onto his back. Tori now pushes Uke's right elbow across his body, with his left hand, to hold Uke there and with his right elbow strikes a blow in Uke's solar plexus.

Figure 140

They resume their normal positions.

5. Ushiro Dori

Uke now arises and comes round behind Tori to kneel on his left knee, catching Tori around the shoulders.

Figure 141

Tori catches Uke's left arm in his right hand as if to do the shoulder throw, and thrusts his right leg as far back between Uke's legs as possible.

Figure 142

Tori now rolls to his left, which takes Uke over his left shoulder onto his back. By continuing his own turn, Tori is able to hold Uke down with his right arm across his body, and to punch him in the testicles with his left fist.

Figure 143

They resume the kneeling position. Tori remains there, and Uke arises and goes to the end of the kata line where he has left his weapons. He kneels ceremoniously, picks up his dagger, and conceals it inside his jacket on his left side. He now returns to kneel in front of Tori.

6. Tsuki Komi

Uke comes up on his toes, and drawing the dagger, takes it back to behind his right hip, ready for a straight thrust forwards at Tori's stomach. As he makes the thrust, he raises his left knee and steps forward on his left foot. Tori's first move must be to swivel on his left knee, taking his right back to behind the axis of the kata, and raising his right knee. This takes him out of the way of the thrust, which passes harmlessly in front of him.

The other movements are exactly as for the stomach punch, described in number 2. Tori catches Uke's right elbow with his left and pulls him onto a punch between the eyes with his right fist.

Figure 144

He now changes hands, catches Uke's right wrist with his right and puts his left hand over Uke's left shoulder to catch his right lapel. So he is able to apply the stomach armlock and the stranglehold.

Figure 145

They return to the kneeling position facing each other.

7. Kiri Komi

Uki again takes the dagger in his right hand, and raises it above his head for a direct downcut at Tori's head.

Figure 146

As he makes the cut, Uke rises on his toes and raises his right knee to step forward with that foot. Again, Tori's first move must be to take his whole body behind the line of the kata, towards which this downcut is being made. He comes up on his toes, swivels on his left knee, and raising his right, he takes it back behind the line of the kata. At the same time he catches Uke's wrist in both his hands, bears his left elbow down on Uke's right elbow, and so applies a straight armlock to Uke's right arm.

Figure 147

To make this armlock effective, Tori must twist Uke's arm so that the elbow is uppermost.

Uke will submit, and they resume their positions facing each other. Then, for the next movement, Uke arises, and comes to Tori's right side, and kneels down about eight inches away, and slightly in advance of Tori, facing the same way as Tori, that is down the line of the kata.

8. Yoko Tsuki

With his dagger in his right hand, drawn back to his right hip, Uke turns towards Tori and makes a thrust at Tori's right side.

Figure 148

To avoid this, Tori must make a three-quarter turn by taking his right leg back and around and coming up onto his right foot. He swivels on his left knee. This results in the thrust passing in front of him. As he turns he catches Uke's right arm at the elbow, as before and pulls him onto a right handed punch between the eyes.

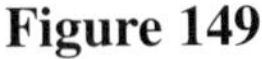

Figure 149

He then changes hands, and holding Uke's right wrist in his right arm and putting his left over Uke's left shoulder to catch his right lapel, he applies the stomach armlock and stranglehold combined, as in Number 6.

Figure 150

Uke submits and sheaths his dagger. Both Tori and Uke arise to their feet. Tori remains still at his position on the kata line. Uke goes to the far end, kneels down, first to the high kneeling position, then on both knees, and lays down his dagger exactly where it lay before. He then arises, first to the high kneeling position, and then to his feet, and turns to face Tori ready for the second set, which comprises twelve standing attacks.

SET TWO (Attacks Standing)

1. Ryote Dori.
Uke advances and catches Tori's wrists as before, right wrist in left hand, left wrist in right hand, thumbs inside.

Figure 151

Tori parts his arms slightly to bring Uke off balance forwards, and kicks him in the testicles with the ball of his right foot. Be careful not to actually land the kick.

Figure 152

Tori now opens his right hand and turning to his left by taking his left foot back, he catches Uke's left wrist in both his hands. He is now facing across the kata axis, and if he bears down on Uke's left elbow with his right, he will apply a straight armlock.

Figure 153

Uke submits, and is released.

2. Sode Tori
Uke comes to Tori's left side, and catching his sleeve at the left elbow forces him to take three steps forwards. Both begin with the right foot and move in tsugiashi.

Figure 154

As Uke is making his third step with his right, Tori stops and delivers a kick at his right knee with the little-toe edge of his left foot. This causes Uke to bend his knee slightly.

Figure 155

Tori immediately turns, by replacing his left foot on the ground and swivelling on it, pulls Uke's right sleeve towards the ground, and pushes back on Uke's left shoulder with his right hand, so bringing Uke off balance backwards, and making it possible to throw him with O Soto Gari, the outer reaping throw.

Figure 156

3. Tsuki Kake

Uke arises and comes to face Tori again. Taking his right fist back to his hip, he makes a direct blow at Tori's face, stepping forwards with his right foot as he does so.

Figure 157

Tori makes the usual evasion, by taking his right foot back, so that he is behind the kata line and the blow passes in front of him. He blocks it downwards with his right hand and places his left on Uke's right shoulder.

Figure 158

As Uke reacts to this by straightening up, Tori lets his right hand slide up Uke's right arm and across the front of his throat. He quickly steps behind Uke and with his left hand catches his own right wrist, and pulls the arm tight against Uke's throat, in the Naked stranglehold, Ushiro jime. It is important that the bone on the thumb side of Tori's forearm is in contact with Uke's throat to have the maximum effect and that he unbalances Uke backwards.

Figure 159

Uke submits and Tori releases him.

4. Tsugi Ashi

Uke comes forwards until he is one pace from Tori. He then tries to deliver an uppercut with his right hand. Tori takes his head back so that it passes harmlessly up in front of his chin.

Figure 160

Tori catches Uke's wrist, his left hand below his right, in both hands, and turns by taking his right foot back in three quarters of a circle. This brings him with his back to Uke's right side, and Uke's right arm under his armpit.

Figure 161

Now, by pressing down on the elbow with his armpit and raising the wrist, Tori can apply a straight armlock. He must ensure that the elbow is uppermost, by turning Uke's wrist.

Figure 162

Uke will submit and Tori releases him.

5. Suri Age

Uke now stands a pace away, and with the heel of his right hand, makes a thrust at Tori's chin. The object is to jerk Tori's head back and to injure his neck.

Figure 163

Tori takes his head back to avoid, and deflects the attack upwards with his open left hand. At the same time he punches Uke in the solar plexus with his right fist.

Figure 164

This causes Uke to double up, forwards, and Tori uses this advantage to step in with his left foot, pass his left arm round Uke's back, and perform the Hip Throw (O Goshi) to Uke's left.

Figure 165

6. Yoke Uchi

They return to a position with Uke one pace away. Uke swings his right fist back and aims a blow at Tori's left temple with the bottom of the fist. He advances his right foot as he does so.

Figure 166

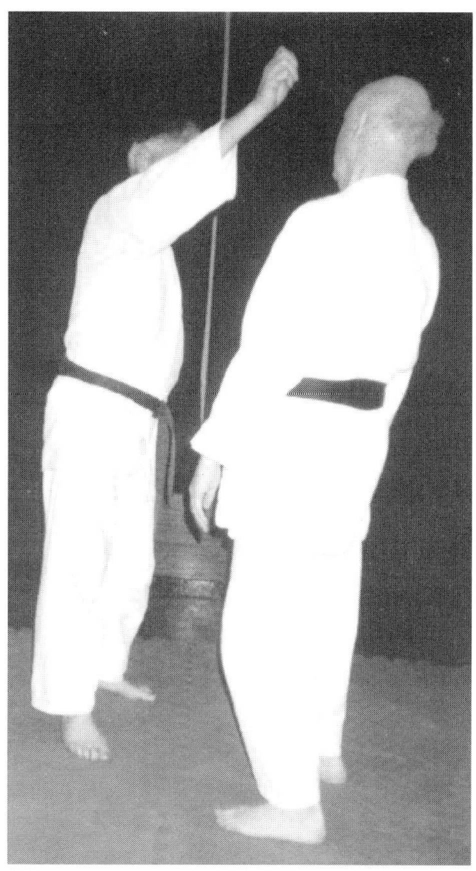

Tori lowers his head to avoid, and steps to his left with his left foot. At the same time, he catches Uke's left lapel with his right hand, thumb inside.

Figure 167

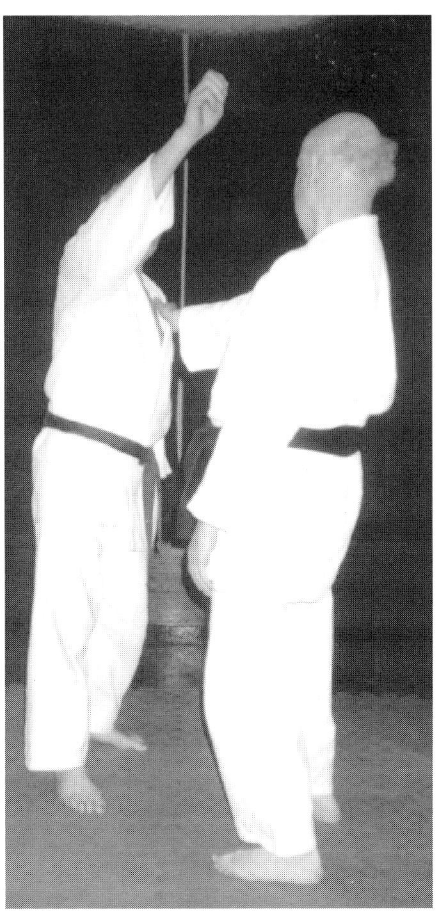

He now quickly moves behind Uke, passes his left hand over Uke's left shoulder and grabs his right lapel with the left hand. He is now in a position to apply the sliding collar stranglehold, (Okuri eri).

Figure 168

He must take Uke off balance backwards as he does so, by stepping back slightly.

7. Ke Age

Tori and Uke are facing each other. Uki tries to kick Tori in the testicles with his right foot.

Tori makes a quarter turn to his right, by taking his right foot back, so that the kick will pass harmlessly in front of him.

Figure 169

Tori now catches Uke's ankle in both his hands, and stepping back to face Uke, he kicks him in the same way with his right foot.

Figure 170

8. Ushiro Dori.

Uke goes around to stand behind Tori. They both advance three short steps beginning with the right foot. On his third step forwards, Uke seizes Tori around the shoulders with both hands.

Figure 171

Tori immediately drops onto his right knee, and catches Uke's right arm, inserting his right shoulder deep under Uke's right armpit. He is thus able to do the shoulder throw from a kneeling position on Uke.

Figure 172

When Uke has fallen, Tori controls him with his left handed hold on the sleeve, and strikes Uke at the base of his nose with the little finger edge of the right hand, one of the atemi-waza.

Figure 173

9. Tsuki Komi

Uke now goes to the end of the kata line, where he has left his weapons, kneels down and picks up his dagger, as in the preparation for Number 6 of Set One.

Stepping forward with his left foot, he takes the dagger back to his hip for a thrust at Tori's stomach. As he thrusts he lunges forward with his right foot.

Tori makes the quarter turn (Tai sabaki) by taking his right foot back, swivelling on his left, so that he is behind the line of the kata and parallel to the thrust, which goes harmlessly past him.

Figure 174

At the same time, Tori catches Uke's right elbow and pulls him forward with his left hand, onto a punch between the eyes delivered with his right fist.

Figure 175

Tori now changes hands, holds Uke's right wrist with his right, and passes his left hand over Uke's left shoulder to seize his right lapel. He is thus able to do the stomach armlock and stranglehold seen before in this kata.

Figure 176

Uke submits.

10. Kiri Komi

Uke now raises the dagger, held in his right hand, high above his head for a direct downcut at Tori's head.

Figure 177

Tori again makes the quarter turn by taking his right foot back, so that the cut will pass in front of him. Uke has stepped forward with his right foot when making the cut. Tori now catches Uke's right wrist in both his hands, takes his left shoulder over Uke's arm, and by bearing down with his shoulder and lifting with his hands, he applies a straight armlock to Uke's right arm. It is essential that Uke's elbow is turned uppermost, and Tori should step across with his left foot so that the line of his feet makes a T-shape with the line of Uke's feet.

Figure 178

11. Nuki Kake

Tori stands perfectly still in his place, whilst Uke goes to the place where he has left his sword. He kneels down ceremoniously, high kneeling position first, then on both knees, toes extended, and lays down his dagger. He picks up the sword, right hand on the hilt, left hand on the scabbard, and stands it on its point, before putting it in his belt on his left-hand side. Usually the swords have a string attached to the scabbard, with which he ties it to his belt. He now arises to the high kneeling position, then gets up, and approaches Tori.

Holding the scabbard in his left hand, and the hilt with his right, he steps forward with his right foot, and makes to draw the sword.

Figure 179

Tori steps forward with his right foot, and with his right wrist he blocks the attempted draw.

Figure 180

He now steps behind Uke, allowing his right hand to pass under Uke's and to slide up behind his neck, and passing his left hand over Uke's left shoulder to seize his right lapel. He pulls Uke slightly off balance backwards, and applies the stranglehold described in Number 4 of set 2 of Katame No Kata.

Figure 181

Uke submits. He then sheathes his sword, and stands at a distance of about twelve feet from Tori.

12. Kiri Oroshi

Uke unsheathes his sword, preparatory to making a direct downcut at Tori's head. There is a precise method of unsheathing, which is an art in itself. First, Uke steps forward with his right foot, then, as his left is advancing, he starts to unsheathe the sword at the moment when the left foot is passing the right. He turns the sheath with his left hand, so that the flat side of the sword is to the ground, and the curvature is away from his body. When the sword is half-way out, he turns the sheath still further so that the cutting edge is pointing upwards, and completes the draw. He now brings his right foot in line with his left, and at this point, the sword is held in his right hand only, with the point directed at Tori's throat.

As Uke is unsheathing in this way, Tori retreats two steps, left and right, and stands facing Uke.

Figure 182

Stepping forward with his left foot, Uke raises the sword directly above his head, with both hands, and then stepping forward with his right, he brings it down with a direct cut at the top of Tori's head. Tori makes the quarter turn (Tai Sabaki) by taking his right foot back, so that the cut passes harmlessly in front of him.

Tori catches his right wrist with his right hand, pulling him forward off balance, and passes his left hand over Uke's left shoulder to seize his right lapel. He can thus do the usual armlock and stranglehold. There is no punch between the eyes on this occasion.

Figure 183

Uke now sheathes his sword, in the exactly opposite way to the drawing. The sword is held with the edge uppermost as it is inserted into the scabbard, and turned to blade flat and edge pointing away from Uke when half-way in. When the sword is completely sheathed, the curvature is upwards.

Tori now remains in his own position perfectly still, while Uke goes to the end of the kata, turns his back on Tori, kneels down and ceremoniously lays down his sword. He now picks up, first dagger, then sword, placing them first in his left hand, then transferring them to his right, and gets up, first to the high kneeling position, then to his feet. He comes towards Tori and stops at a distance of twelve feet. The curvature of the sword must be upwards, and the dagger held nearest to his body.

Together, Tori and Uke kneel, first to the high kneeling position, then on both knees, toes extended for the kneeling bow. Uke lays down his sword and dagger for this, exactly as at the beginning of the kata, but when they arise for the standing bow to the joseki, the curvature of the sword is downwards. This is the only time in the kata when this is so.

FINAL POINTS

When studying kata, it is best to work with the same partner, so that you become accustomed to each other's movements.

If you are using weapons, as in Kime No Kata, it is particularly important that you demonstrate with your usual partner, with whom you will have built up confidence through familiarity with his movements.

First, learn the sequence, splitting the kata into sections, if you wish, and learning one section at a time, until you know the complete kata, then polish up each individual movement with repetition, thousands of times. This is vital in tai sabaki, the turn that will take you out of danger from a punch or a stab. It looks so simple to make this quarter turn, but to do it correctly and with simplicity and to time it right demands practice.

When you have learnt a kata as Tori, change over with your partner and learn it as Uke. If you aspire to become a teacher, you will need to know it both ways.

For safety's sake, always use imitation weapons in practice. Some performers never use the real weapons, though it is customary for high grades to do so on ceremonial occasions. If you use real weapons at such a time, only do so with your regular partner.

When you practise, think of the reasons why you are performing a movement in the way you are. Try to understand the principles behind it. Aim at the simplest way, remembering Dr.Kano's dictum" Maximum Efficiency-Minimum Effort." Cultivate calmness, and stillness of body and mind. Be relaxed.

Ju-jitsu was never intended for aggression, but purely for self-defence. It relied on turning the impetus of an opponent's attack to his disadvantage, and this impetus was an important factor in enabling the weak to overcome the strong. If there was no attack, then no response would be needed. This principle is clearly seen in the katas, and is the basis of traditional judo. Of course, in contest judo, an attacking style in encouraged, since if both were defensive nothing would happen. But though necessary if the art is to become a sport, the aggressiveness thus developed is a departure from the basic principles of ju-jitsu, on which judo is based.

Over the years, minor variations have crept into the katas, and efforts to standardise them have failed, even in Japan. It is best to think of the sequence as a musical score which different performers will interpret slightly differently, even though they are playing the same notes. The sequence, like the musical notation , never changes. No-one disputes this. But as you study to understand what you are doing and why, and as you try to simplify your movements, you will evolve your own interpretation of the kata, and in doing so, you will gain a deeper insight into judo.